It's All About Worship

It's All About Worship
A Journey to the Heart of God Through Worship

Copyright © 2024 Michael and Meredith Mauldin

Unless otherwise noted, Scriptures are taken from The Holy Bible, English Standard Version® (ESV®), copyright © 2001 by Crossway, a publishing ministry of Good News Publishers. Used by permission. All rights reserved. | Scripture quotations marked NIV are taken from the HOLY BIBLE, NEW INTERNATIONAL VERSION®, Copyright © 1973, 1978, 1984, 2011 International Bible Society. Used by permission of Zondervan. All rights reserved.

This book is set in the typeface *Athelas* designed by Veronika Burian and Jose Scaglione.

Paperback ISBN: 978-1-955546-65-2

A Publication of *Tall Pine Books*
119 E Center Street, Suite B4A | Warsaw, Indiana 46580
www.tallpinebooks.com

| 1 24 24 20 16 02 |

Published in the United States of America

IT'S ALL ABOUT WORSHIP

A Journey to the Heart of God Through Worship

Michael and Meredith Mauldin

"The Mauldin's have been close friends of the Miller's for the last 15 years. Our view of worship has been deeply impacted and shaped by their lives and revelation. The pages of this book define their pursuit of Jesus and have been lived out for almost 2 decades. My prayer is that this message will impact you as much as it has impacted me. Thank you Michael and Meredith for making it *all about worship*."

—MICHAEL MILLER
Founder & Pastor *UPPERROOM*

"I love how the Mauldins live with bold humility and this book powerfully captures and communicates all that they carry. The relational tone of the book helps make the truth applicable, possible, and enjoyable. My worship has grown because my awe and wonder of God has increased from reading how God spoke and moved in their lives. This is my new favorite book on worship and I believe it will shape the next season of the Church!"

—DEREK HARDEN
Pastor at *Christ Fellowship* and Co-Founder of *True You Leader* Church, Kingsport, TN

"Just finished reading *It's All About Worship*! And I'm so proud of Michael and Meredith! I've known the Mauldins for over a decade and have experienced much of this book with them.

I was leading worship with Meredith the night the cloud appeared during service. These are not just words on pages; this is a collection of God encounters and the Biblical lessons learned through them. If you desire to know Him more, this book is a must read. Well done!"

—TRAES HOWARD
Chief Levite, Director of *UPPERROOM School of Ministry*

"Loving Jesus is life's greatest achievement. Worship is simply an expression of our love and honor for Jesus. His Presence is life itself. Since I was a young boy, I have found true, Spirit led worship to be a direct and consistent path into His manifest Presence. I have shared many such moments with Michael and Meredith Mauldin. We were all marked by the beauty of the Lord over the years. This is a treasure from Heaven. The Mauldins have radically pursued the Lord so beautifully for years and it is an honor to know them and their children. May the Lord Jesus birth a desire to adore Him as He deserves to be as you read this book."

—MICHAEL KOULIANOS
Pastor, *Jesus Image*

"I can't express enough how grateful I am for The Mauldin's. They truly practice what they preach not just creatively but also relationally. I deeply trust Michael and Meredith.

The revelation they have on worship has significantly changed my life, my songwriting and my worship leading. If like me, you're looking to learn how to worship Jesus in spirit and in truth I encourage you to read this book and soak in these words. You will be so glad you did."

—ELYSSA SMITH
UPPERROOM Dallas

"This is more than a book about worship, much more. It's an invitation."

—RAY HUGHES
Author of *Sound of Heaven, Symphony of Earth*
Florence, Alabama

Before we begin, I want to give thanks. Thank You Jesus for the incredible journey we've been on to get to know You more. You truly know our hearts desires and fulfill them in ways that continually blow our minds! We were made for adventure and following You is the greatest adventure the world has ever known. This book is dedicated to You!

CONTENTS

FOREWORD

66 **I**T'S NOT ABOUT *what* you're saying, as much as it is about *who* is saying it." My husband, Michael, has said this to me often before I get up to speak. This is his way of reminding me that our lives ought to convey the message we are carrying. When we embody our message, it comes with not only knowledge, but authority. Messages that change lives are ones that are lived out by the messenger.

You hold in your hand such a message. This message is a life lived, a message embodied.

I remember vividly the first time I saw Michael and Meredith Mauldin (18 years ago at the time of this writing). I noticed them before I was introduced to them. These two are hard not to notice. As you'll read in the following pages, they both had careers in acting and modeling. They are noticeable. It is not everyday you see two tall, stunning people walk into church with such unassuming demeanors. They came to a worship night at our church, and I distinctly remember Meredith worshiping unabashedly. She was free, extravagant, and exuberant in her worship. Who was this beautiful blonde who was lost in worship to her King?

Call me creepy, but I used to watch people worship. In that particular season, I was new to this world—I myself was learning how to worship, and I was especially intrigued by people who seemed to believe that they were communing with a real God as they worshiped. Though a depth of intimacy can't be measured by expression, it certainly communicates something—especially when that expression is consistent over the times and seasons, the ups and downs of life.

As the kindness of God would have it, Meredith and I eventually became very close friends. We were, and are, knit at heart by a mutual love and hunger for Jesus. For a few precious years, we lived just blocks from each other. Weekly, sometimes daily, we did the mundane things of life together—we folded each oth-

er's laundry, prepped food, worked out together—all
while our kids played together in the backyard or made
up dances and shows. What made those times anything but mundane was the conversation over laundry
baskets and chopping boards. We talked about Jesus,
Scripture, prayer, and worship, worship, worship. We
could talk for hours! Thank God for eternally weighty
friendship!

Meredith and Michael gifted our UPPERROOM
community with an unapologetic face-like-flint pursuit of true praise and worship. They refused to go
through the motions, or accept something because
"that's what every other church does." They refused
mediocrity, tradition, and lukewarmness. God had
provoked them with an invitation and a declaration:
"It's all about worship!" And they have been relentless
in responding to Him and His invitation.

Much of what you may know of our precious UP-
PERROOM worship today came from Meredith's tire-
less determination to birth what God had conceived
in her and Michael's hearts. They have never changed
the tune, single heartedly pursuing an honest, biblical,
and wholehearted offering to the One who is unimag-
inably more worthy than we can know. The Mauldins
have an extraordinary ability to see gold in an unculti-

vated worshiper and help develop them into a mature, risk-taking, and genuine worship leader.

Perhaps my favorite part of this manuscript is the invitation to all, regardless of vocation. This is a book that isn't just for worship leaders in the traditional sense, but for the pastor, the mom, the business leader, the photographer. Michael and Meredith have invited us all into the beauty of true worship. I pray you'll be provoked, equipped, and empowered to worship Jesus as never before.

> *"Here's the one thing I crave from Yahweh, the one thing I seek above all else: I want to live with him every moment in his house, beholding the marvelous beauty of Yahweh, filled with awe, delighting in his glory and grace. I want to contemplate in his temple."* (Psalms 27:4 TPT)

—LORISA MILLER
Co-Founder and Senior Leader of *UPPERROOM*

INTRODUCTION

CUE SPOTLIGHT: A tall blonde woman stands in the middle of a large stage. She's wearing a beautiful long black dress, and a 16-piece orchestra in tuxedos glitter the stage behind her. The venue buzzes with people dressed to the nines waiting to dance and enjoy the music that would bring them back to a time gone by. In between crystal chandeliers and fancy hotel ballrooms, she sings and mimics another era effortlessly.

Then, it's onto the next gig. She changes her clothes as she changes her scenery, and it's short shirts and tight pants now. Time to learn dance choreography, pop beats, and vocal runs to try to prove that she can also make it in the pop world. Dance, give it all you have, sell an audience, entertain! Work hard, sweat hard, sing hard! Tour bus, costume changes, late nights.

Though I'm sure you've caught on by now, I'll let you in completely: that blonde was me.

The trunk of my car looked more like a closet, filled to the brim with my actor headshot, resume, and clothing changes of all kinds. I was ready to walk into an audition for a commercial or movie at any time. During the day, I was an actress. The evenings were reserved for music rehearsals and gigs.

All I had ever known was performance, and honestly, it's what drove me! How far could I go? I craved the attention, and when I was doing well, I was up. But when I didn't book the job, I was down. That's the rollercoaster of performance—exciting and volatile.

But, as suddenly as my gig life seemed to have come together, all of the lights were gone. I found myself freezing in a dark room in the Middle Eastern country of Turkey, sitting alone by a wood-burning stove. Crying, I thought to myself, *What in the world am I doing here?*

* * *

I'm Meredith Mauldin, and my husband, Michael, and I will be writing this book together since we both carry pieces and parts that bring a fuller picture. We both have different styles of writing and unique perspectives on worship, but God made us one, so having us both tell our story, you will get a more complete perspective!

This book is based on 17 years of asking the question, "What does it look like to worship you, Jesus?" We have found that so much of this process is so simple that we totally miss it. Yet, in that simplicity, we've found it to be even more profound. We've had to become like little children again, completely captivated by everything our Father does, speaks, and creates.

We hope this little book on our pursuit of what it looks like to worship will completely ruin you for anything less than lavish gratitude and praise that leads to intimate worship. As my husband says, "We want to bring the fun back into fundamentals!"

First, we want to give you the story behind the discovery. We both have pieces that are important context for the revelation, of course, but also, who doesn't love a great story?! After that, we'll dive into the biblical background and foundations. But we won't just give you information, we'll teach you practical ways to implement it. Honestly, we can all agree that Christians don't need more head knowledge. If we would just implement even 20% of what we already know, the world would be flipped upside down. So, the practical implementation is of utmost importance to us.

At the end of a few of the chapters, you'll find exercises that you can do alone, in a small group, or even with your church. The best way to learn and really have it stick is by doing. After all, Jesus made His disciples learn by doing!

Alright, let's do this!

1

IT'S ALL ABOUT WORSHIP

NOW, BEFORE YOU read that chapter title and say, "It's not all about worship; it's all about Jesus!" Yes, I agree. But the question always remains in this life with every decision we make, "Who will be worshipped?" Our life, our time, and our money spent all reflect what and who we worship.

This story takes you on our journey the Lord initiated with an awakening. Yes, I mean a literal awakening. Michael and I had been married less than six months and were living in Hollywood, CA hoping to be lights in the entertainment industry. We were lying asleep in bed one early morning when Michael sat up abruptly and loudly yelled, "IT'S ALL ABOUT WOR-SHIP!"

I was jolted awake, utterly confused as to what just happened. Looking over at him, I knew he was a bit bewildered as well. Still, he repeated again—much quieter this time, I might add—"it's all about worship."

He began to pace around the apartment, pondering what he had just said. The atmosphere was pregnant with Heaven and awe and wonder, and I was almost as shaken up as he was. It was as if time was at a standstill, and God was extending His hand toward us, inviting us into a journey to discover what that phrase truly meant.

Later that morning, we were walking around the perimeter of the Paramount Studios lot in West Hollywood. It was a walk we often did together because our small condo faced the large stone fence that kept the public from snooping on the movies and TV shows that were being filmed. That day, our walk was filled with a different conversation than the usual talk of auditions, acting class, and next steps in the entertainment world. Instead, there seemed to be a heavenly invitation that we didn't have words for, but somehow, we knew we needed to pursue it.

We really didn't know what that invitation meant

at the time. Michael was a new believer, so he thought worship was singing a couple songs in church, and he didn't really have a clue as to why we even did that. Maybe you find yourself thinking the same thing, if you're really honest. But that was all about to change.

This single "awakening" started us on a lifelong journey of what it truly means to worship God. Jesus said that the Father is seeking "worshippers." (John 4:23) If God is seeking worshippers, then worship must be important to Him, right? And we know that worshipping Him in spirit and in truth here and now is just the tip of the iceberg. If worship surrounds His glorious throne, and we will worship Him for eternity... then I'm sure we can never exhaust the subject!

I'll Think About It

I've often found when the Lord drops something into your spirit—like the phrase "it's all about worship"—it truly is an invitation. In this particular revelation, the understanding was not immediately there for us. It has unfolded over time, and it is still unfolding today!

At that time, I was a believer, but my vocation was singing and acting in the secular world. I had absolutely no interest in pursuing "Christian music" or what I knew at the time to be "worship music." God was dropping hints, maybe even blaring messages to me about my calling, but at the time, I had blinders on to keep my focus on the pursuit of the entertainment world.

I remember sitting on the couch one day when the phone rang.

A deep, scratchy smoker's voice greeted me from the other end. "Meredith, I've been thinking about you."

I knew the voice well. It was the rough, no-non-sense, shoot-you-straight voice of Lee Peterson, my manager. She had smoked for most of her life, and if you had never met her, you probably would have thought she was a man when you heard her speak on the phone. It didn't help that her name could go either way!

She had given her life to God in her later years, which was awesome. Typically, when I heard her voice on the other line it was usually to talk through audition prep or meetings she had booked for me. But this time, she said something I would have never seen coming.

"Meredith, I think you should record some hymns or something. You should make a Christian album."

Thankfully, she couldn't see through the phone to catch my eyeroll and fake smile. "I'll think about it," I said cordially.

For one, you didn't say "no" to Lee Peterson. That would cause a much longer argument than I was in the mood for. But two, I didn't quite know what to fully make of it. As soon as I hung up the phone, I told Michael.

"You'll never believe this. She told me to record some hymns or something. No thanks," I said, annoyed at the mere thought of it.

You see, she was giving me a message that I wasn't ready to accept, but for some reason, I still couldn't stop thinking about it. And it wasn't just Michael that was wrestling through the literal wake-up call that came the morning he shot out of bed.

That little phrase "it's all about worship" sparked something inside me, too, and the conversation with Lee made it all the more real. The phrase wasn't something that we understood logically (head knowledge), but it was something that resonated in our spirits enough to cause a deep hunger to know more. While we didn't know where to go from there, we found God faithful to drop little crumbs and clues for us to follow down the path of discovery.

And let me tell you, oftentimes, the journey with Him becomes more valuable than the discovery itself!

What you hold in your hands is a revelation the Lord gave to us that we hope will be a revelation to you. We want to see the Bride understand worship in an entirely life-altering way, and we pray that what we've learned over the years will be a resource to you. And most of all, we pray that you would encounter the One it is all about.

Lord, let this book point to You. May Your Bride be forever enamored in awe with the beauty of who You are and what You have done.

You Have to Make a Choice

I was raised in a vibrant church consisting of a bunch of young families who had a sincere hunger for the Lord. The church was also super creative, boasting a theater company and dance studio. You could always find me at the theater for rehearsals and performances, and I loved every minute of it!

My parents deeply loved Jesus, and I grew up hearing testimonies of miracles the Lord had done in their lives. Tragically, my father died at the age of 28 in a hunting accident. I was only 2 at the time. Still,

I remember asking Jesus into my life at the age of 3. I didn't really know it then, but as I look back, I can say without question that God is truly a Father to the fatherless. He really did Father me. All that to say, I always had an awareness of Jesus and sincerely wanted to follow him.

My mother remarried when I was 6, and for a myriad of reasons, we didn't stay in that church nor go to church that often at all. (One of my brothers had down syndrome and was a handful, and most churches were sadly not able to handle special needs kids.) During that time, I would go to the Baptist church with my friend from school.

In high school, I started taking a theater class, mainly because I didn't make the volleyball team, and I was immediately hooked. I look back and am just as thankful for shut doors as I am for open ones because they both opened my heart back up to creativity. I started to live and breathe everything music and theater.

When I was just 16 years old, I auditioned for a 16-piece orchestra. First, I was asked to memorize a song from a random recording that wouldn't be the same arrangement or key that the band would play it in. Then, I would be joining the orchestra live on stage in front of a large audience. There was no rehearsal, no prep, and if I made a mistake, the band couldn't follow me because they were all reading the music in front of them.

I was a high school girl with no experience thrown into the deep end to try to swim with 16 professional male musicians in tuxedos with disapproving faces. When it came time to audition, my hand shook so badly I could barely hold the microphone, and I couldn't hear myself sing above the trumpet section blaring behind me. Still, I tried to sing and get through the song, but it didn't go well in my eyes. I hurried off the stage in tears, embarrassed that I had failed miserably, especially in front of so many people.

For whatever reason, the band director thought I had potential and ended up hiring me anyway. I ended up being the female singer for that orchestra for eight years! I sang in high-end ballrooms, bars I wasn't old enough to get into, Republican conventions, fancy New Year's Eve parties, and high-end hotel restaurants. This particular orchestra was even the featured band for cruise ships! It was quite the experience for a teenage girl.

In addition to singing, I continued to audition and

book roles in local theaters and walked through any open doors that came my way.

One day after a rehearsal, one of my theater directors told me that there was a cartoon looking for female voices and suggested that my friend Laura and I go audition. Because I was eager for any opportunities, I was interested right away. So, I asked Laura and we decided to brave the audition together.

The moment we pulled up to the massive, old brown bank building, we both looked at each other with wide eyes, glad we didn't go alone. We walked into a small room that had a large desk with two big computers that you could barely walk by. Behind the desk were two casually dressed guys and an old sound booth with lots of that squishy egg carton stuff in it for soundproofing. We were auditioning for an Anime cartoon I had never heard of before called *Dragon Ball Z*. To my surprise, I ended up booking the voice of a villain character named Android 18. To this day, I still think they typecast me because I kind of look like the character!

At the time, I had no idea that cartoon would one day become the *Mickey Mouse* of the Anime world. Big doors were opening, and I was running through them.

During my second semester of community college, I finally got a talent agent. I booked my first audition for a commercial and was offered a touring show band gig with a salary! I was on cloud nine.

That year, I was taking a college algebra class for the second time. I had quit the class the semester before and had made the excuse that it was too many academic classes for me to keep up with at once. But in all honesty, I just hated algebra and watched the clock like it would walk off the wall. After class one day, I stayed after to talk to the teacher.

"I've just been asked to tour with a really popular show band! I am probably going to miss quite a few days of class traveling all over the nation!" I said excitedly, hoping she would be impressed. However, her expression didn't change.

So, I continued, "And... I was wondering if you might be willing to work with me to figure out how to balance this class and the tour?"

"No," she shot back sternly. "You need to make a choice. You either choose college or this band.'

With that, I flashed her a smile, said goodbye, and walked out of the classroom knowing I wasn't going back. Up to this point, I hadn't really made a choice. I had just been naively exploring something I enjoyed.

Now, a line had been drawn in the sand, and I chose a side. I was going for it!

I quit college and started touring. At the time, I also started writing music, booking commercials and independent films, and booking more voiceovers for cartoons. I loved it, and the pursuit was exhilarating. I never questioned if acting and music were what I was called to do or not. I just knew I was all in!

Do I Even Have a Testimony?

I had a good foundation in the Lord from childhood, but I wouldn't say I had truly encountered Jesus at that point in my life. I stayed out of trouble, but I was gone every weekend touring and had very few good influences around me. I was beginning to test the waters, and, as he likes to do, the enemy started to put questions in my mind like, "Is that really what God said?"

I began to question the Lord's character, and sin started not looking half bad. That scared me. I decided I needed to take a break from the road and get back into church. A friend of mine said he was willing to go to church with me if it was non-traditional, so I literally opened up a phone book (yes, those were still around, and yes, I'm dating myself) and skimmed through the names of churches looking for something unconventional. My finger stopped at a church called God Inc.

"Huh? What kind of denomination is a church called God Inc.?" I spouted out, slightly entertained by the name. My friend was a bartender and particularly interested in business, but not so much God. He really liked that "inc." part, so we decided we would try it out the next Sunday.

It had been quite some time since I had been to church. That morning, I think I found a jean skirt that was probably too short and too tight for the setting, but at least I was going! We got in the car and headed toward the address we found in the phone book, totally unsure of what to expect. We pulled up to a run-down strip mall center, which, thankfully, had a sign out front that let us know the place was real and not a joke. So, we hesitantly walked in.

At the door, the pastor, Terry Weir, greeted me with these piercing Jesus eyes and proceeded to say things to me that very few people, if anyone, could have known about me. He said it all very casually like it was an everyday conversation, but what he was saying felt like answers to questions I had only pondered with God. I was stunned as I'd never experienced that happen before. He spoke out dozens of things he could have never known unless God had told him directly.

Pastor Terry had been a photographer in NYC in the high fashion industry. In the evenings, he used to walk the streets on what was considered the danger-ous side of town and minister to teens who were prob-ably up to no good. He and his wife had crazy testimo-nies! While in NYC, they had felt called to move back to Dallas to start that small church with the strange name—which they later changed. I believe that church with its crazy name was just for me. God provided a fa-ther for me through Terry, whom I desperately need-ed in that time of questioning. And, praise God, my friend accepted Jesus in that season, too!

God was calling me in a new way. He was pulling me in and giving me a hunger I hadn't known before. I had been in church growing up, and I was all about being moral and doing the right thing, but suddenly everything felt different. I'll never forget the moment I was sitting in a pew of an old church with stained glass windows listening to a young preacher speak to a young singles' group. He talked about the story of Jacob and how he wrestled with God. Naturally, the pastor asked us if we were willing to wrestle 'til we en-countered God like Jacob did. I was completely challenged and convicted. It was as if a lightbulb turned on, and a thought that had never crossed my mind came in.

Did I ever care enough to want to truly encounter God for myself? Was this my faith, or my parents' faith? Did I have a testimony?

That next morning, I found the nearest park to my house and walked around and around, pleading with God. "I've heard the stories of miracles you did for my parents and miracles of the Bible, but I can't recount any for myself. I have believed that You're real but I don't know what it's like to have an active moment-by-moment relationship. How has this not even occurred to me?!"

From that day on, a new awareness of Jesus in my life began. The spark was lit, and the Holy Spirit made me hungry for more.

The LoveShack

At 23, during one of the busiest times of my life, a very tall, dark, and handsome actor strutted into an acting job that I was booked on the regular. RadioShack, which we now affectionately call the "LoveShack," booked the same few actors to do their in-house training videos monthly. So, anyone new to our talent agency would be booked as an extra.

As Michael walked by, I gave my co-worker, Markus, the wide-eyed silent communication of interest. Markus, who was a good friend and protective of me, shot me back a look of disapproval that read "Don't even think about it."

Funny enough, I was paired with Michael in one of the scenes, so we struck up a conversation.

"So, where are you from?" I said, trying to break the ice.

"Well, I was born in Vegas, then moved to Los Angeles, then Tampa, then Houston…" he says, rambling off a few more cities and states.

"Wow, were you an army brat?" I asked.

"No, just a brat."

I was immediately intrigued. Later, he had a conversation with Markus that I was pretending not to overhear. He shared that he had majored in communications in college with a minor in theology (which is quite hilarious because he hadn't even been a believer when he received his minor). Markus was a strong believer and looked my way to shoot me a look that said, "Okay, maybe you can think about it."

Michael will go into detail about what happened later that day in the next chapter, but I want to set the record straight from my side! Yes, he did ask about my CD release party and told me he wanted to go. And I'll admit, I did look up his email to give him the info because I had a gig that night and left the job early. But, I will affectionately deny that I stalked him like he claims so proudly!

I will also admit, like a 6th-grade girl, I went home and looked up his headshot on our talent agency's website and said, "I'm gonna marry that guy!" I'd like to think I was just being prophetic and it just took Michael about four more months to figure that out.

I didn't realize it at the time, but Michael had only been a believer for about a month before we met. But he had truly encountered Jesus and was so hungry for God! He would call me and just ask me to go pray. It was so cute! He would bring me to a park and sit me down as he brought out a candle so we could pray together. He was constantly listening to sermons on the radio or on TV and asked me to fast with him. He just couldn't get enough, and his hunger for God increased my hunger!

I had always heard you needed to be equally yoked to the person you date or marry. What I *thought* that meant was that your partner would need to have been a believer for a similar amount of time. However, real encounter and hunger trumps time, and Michael's insatiable hunger grew him exponentially and, in turn, grew me.

It's Not Your Life Anymore

Again, you'll hear more about this from Michael, but after dating for four months, we were engaged and married shortly after that. We dove headfirst into marriage and, a week after our wedding, packed up and moved across the country to Hollywood, California! I went from running about 100 miles an hour with jobs, gigs, friends and family to a screeching halt with pretty weather, palm trees, and a new husband that I'd only known for seven months.

I had more time on my hands than I had ever known what to do with, and we were hungry to know Jesus and to be "lights in the entertainment world." I devoured every testimony book I could find, and Michael looked for schools of ministry to study at. Soon after we moved, Michael found a run-down church in Gardena, and we started attending there. A fiery South African pastor would preach at that church every morning for the homeless and a few spiritually hungry people like us. Michael would drive there six days a week early in the morning to hear what the pastor was preaching. And every day, no matter what the passage he read was saying, the concluding message was always the same:

"It's not YOUR life anymore! Lay your life down! It is Jesus's life in you!"

In all the years I had been going to church, I had never heard *that* message before. Either I wasn't listening, or it wasn't preached, but after hearing it over and over and over again, it begs you to ask the question, "Am I living *my* life? Or the life *Jesus* has for me?" It was a burning question in our hearts we dared to ask. Shortly after, our lives took a hard left turn that was the wildest, most beautiful and challenging adventure.

Some friends of ours knew Michael was looking into schools, and they suggested looking into YWAM. Michael, being the radical person he is, decided that if he was gonna do that, it should be in the place where Jesus walked. So, we sent an email request to a base in Israel with a Hail Mary prayer that went something like, "Lord, if you would like us to go to this school, you'll have to provide money for us to get there and a sub-renter for our apartment." We had signed a year lease, and had only been there for five months at the time.

A few hours later, Michael received an email back reading *Mailer Daemon: failure to deliver message.* Right as he opened and began to read the error message, another email popped into the inbox confirming our email request to YWAM Israel. *What?!* We weren't sure how it went through, but it did, and we were elated!

Our faith then skyrocketed when my brother, out of the blue, called, saying he wanted to move from Austin, TX, to LA and needed a place to live! With that, Michael called his parents, who were not believers at the time, and announced that he was moving his blonde wife to the Middle East.

Well, that's not actually how he said it, but that's definitely how they heard it! Michael's dad proceeded to tell him that he had lost his mind, asking how we were going to pay for the trip because he knew we didn't have extra money.

When Michael responded with a simple "God will provide," his dad told him he needed to get himself checked into a mental institution. But that didn't stop us!

After that conversation, Michael didn't lose any steam, and we continued to pray and believe God was going to make a way where there was no way. I had just read a book on Brother Andrew, who had crazy testimonies of God providing in miraculous ways by just asking our Father in Heaven. So, instead of writing letters asking for support, we felt strongly like we just needed to pray and believe for the provision.

A week or so later, I received a letter in the mail from the government. If you remember, my earthly father had died in an accident when I was two years old, and I had received death benefit checks until I turned 18. I was now 24, so those checks had stopped 6 years prior. I opened the envelope and, to my massive surprise, there was a letter stating that they had messed up my payments in the past. There, in that same envelope, was a check for $15,000. That moment is forever seared into my memory!

My Father in Heaven (both, actually) supernaturally provided for us to go to Israel for six months to do YWAM. The transition was seamless. My brother moved into our apartment and even took over Michael's personal training job, and we were off to the Middle East.

God made it ever so clear that we were supposed to be there, and I needed that reminder to be sure. If it hadn't been so obvious, I might have left early and

was one of the most challenging and marking times of
my life. I had laid my life down, just like the South African preacher had said to do, but I thought it was tem-
porary. I thought that after the six months were done,
I would just come back to my life as an actor and singer—but with more of God, of course.

You're MY Worshipper

Four months into our YWAM school, as I was sitting
alone in that dark room in Antakya, Turkey, I was coming to grips (or not really coming to grips) with the fact
that all my "gifts and talents" were pretty meaningless
there.

Before we go any further, I want to share this confession:

As I alluded to earlier, I never wanted to sing
"Christian music." It all felt "lesser than" compared to
what I was doing. I remember talking to a good friend
of mine who played drums for an award-winning
Christian artist who told me they were driving around
the country doing youth camps in a beat-up van and
getting paid $75 a gig. I would get paid $500 to sing a
song or two at a local event! There was no way I was

driving around the country for gas money. That was totally underneath me... or so I thought!

Okay, back to freezing in Turkey!

I was sitting there, arms crossed, arguing with God. Once I had been stripped of my fast-paced, busy life, I was faced with myself. It seemed like I had no favor with the local people and was really just a distraction on the mission. Culturally, I wasn't allowed to draw attention to myself, look people in the eye, or leave the house for much more than grocery shopping.

Michael, on the other hand, had a ton of favor. Every time he walked out of the house (that looked more like a bomb shelter with hospital lighting and concrete walls than a house), he would happen to run into crazy, exciting ministry opportunities. Every time I left the house, I was either completely ignored or received ugly comments by teenage boys who had nothing better to do than give the blonde foreigner a hard time.

I cried and wrestled with God because for the last six weeks, I had been feeling the Lord ask me if I would be willing to stay and minister in the Middle East. But why?! I thought I had already been following what he had called me to do! I had 10 years of acting and singing under my belt, and I was finally making headway.

We had moved to LA, where my manager and acting coach said I would book something big in the next pilot season. Why would God want me to stay somewhere I didn't even have a purpose? I didn't understand, and I was more than frustrated—I was downright angry.

So, right there in that moment, shivering in the house with my black puffy coat fully zipped up, sitting by the dying fire in the stove, I bitterly surrendered with tears streaming down my face.

"God, I don't understand. I don't understand at all. BUT I'm willing!"

Suddenly, it was as if time stood still, and everything went into slow motion. It felt as though the wind of another realm swept in. I didn't hear an audible voice, but it was as clear as if it was:

"YOU ARE CALLED TO BE MY WORSHIPPER!"

In that single moment, everything shifted. Immediately, the eyes of my heart were open to the understanding of what was just declared. The King of kings, the highest One of all, had just asked me to sing and worship *Him*. And I came alive.

All the lesser thoughts of stages, crowds, and selfish ambition fell off like scales from my eyes. The magnitude of that simple phrase from the mouth of God changed me forever. Everything from my voice to my desires changed, and peace rushed in where I had been striving. Hope entered where I had been captive to disappointment.

He called me a worshipper that day, and no one can ever take that away from me. Why? Because it wasn't given to me by man, but by God, the One who created me! He called me His worshipper, and that meant that I could worship from a closet in Turkey the exact same way I could on a stage in front of thousands. My audience was One.

That day, I took a deep breath for what felt like the first time. All I wanted to do was worship, but I still didn't know how or what that would look like. Remember, up until that point in my life, all I had known was performance. I had no idea what it meant to truly worship.

But He was about to teach me.

2

THE WAR FOR OUR WORSHIP

Michael

South Beach, Earth: 2001

*A*N INSTANT THRUST *of electricity surged through my body, pinning my back to the cold tile floor. Electric power and love were coursing through me, leaving every hair on my body standing at attention toward their Maker. I was completely and utterly paralyzed under this otherworldly power. Tears rose from the deep and pooled into my eyes. They then began to trickle out of the corners and stream down the outside of my face as I realized I'd encountered something—SomeOne— eternal.*

Okay, before I go deeper into that story, let's back

up a little bit—or more accurately, "a lot bit"—to the year 1993. For a little context, Meredith and I could not have had more opposite backgrounds growing up. My rendition of her testimony is that she gave her life to the Lord at two years old and re-dedicated her life to the Lord at four because, at age three, she'd been caught pillow-fighting her brothers!

Needless to say, Meredith was a good girl. She knew early on in life that she wanted to be a singer and actress when she grew up. It seemed that God's plan was carved out plain and simple for her. My path toward God and His calling on my life was not so clear-cut. It was a winding, arduous road that detoured through hell a few times too many. The only explanation that I have for the reason that I'm still alive today is that God had a plan for my life that even I, in my quest for destruction, could not mess up because His grace was more powerful than my mistakes.

My childhood was not typical, nor were my dreams for the future. Most kids have dreams of being professional athletes, doctors, lawyers, princes and princesses, mothers, and fathers. Not me. As crazy as it may sound, my ultimate dream was to be in a crime family, or as we know it, the Mafia!

I know this is an odd setup for a book about worship, but stay with me. It will make sense shortly! Let me give you an illustrative backstory to set the context for the war on what and who we worship.

Houston, Texas: 1993

The world was mine. I was only 17 at the time; however, I was convinced that I was above it all. My life at that point was cloaked with an illusion of invincibility that led me to make some consistently foolish decisions. I was getting ready to go to the gym, standing there in my boxer shorts after just having put my oversized t-shirt on, when the home phone rang.

"Is Stephen Mauldin there?"

Who is calling me by my first name? I thought. "Who is this?" I said sternly.

"Is Stephen Mauldin there?" the voice repeated.

"Who is this?"

Click. They hung up.

Ten seconds later, there was a thundering at my front door. From my second-story window, I sheepishly peered through the blinds, looking down toward my front porch. My heart skipped a beat as I saw at least five men dressed in black SWAT-style fatigues with assault rifles pointing toward the door.

Holy ***.

"We are being raided!" I yelled to Tony downstairs as I ran to the back bedroom to look out the windows. There I was met with the view of another man in black fatigues scaling over the garage towards my back patio. I ran over to Tony. "What should we do, man?"

"Open the door," he said, matter-of-fact.

Reason came rushing in, and I obliged. I opened the door to a myriad of gun barrels pointed directly at my mug. The first guy grabs me and slams me up against the door while twisting my right arm behind my back with the intent to cuff me right there in my mother's home.

"You are under arrest. You have the right to remain silent, you—"

"For what?"

"Aggravated assault with a deadly weapon."

"I've already been arrested for that," I responded. For a fleeting second, I had a glimmer of hope that this was a mistake. The month before, I had already been arrested for aggravated assault with a deadly weapon.

"It's another one," he responded as every molecule of hope evaporated from by being. My shoulders sank as the handcuffs got tighter.

All of that cocky "the world is mine" confidence was fading fast. For those who don't know, when you

have two felony charges, you can't get out on bond.
The old iron clank was forthcoming, and the illusion
of my life as I knew it was crumbling in a moment's
time.

My parents divorced when I was at the tender age
of four. My father, Steve, who never met his own father, nobly took me in and began to raise me. He was
a bit rough around the edges, having been raised in a
trailer park in desert oil fields of west Texas. A place of
hard men. Needless to say, I didn't have a lot of nurtur-
ing going on, which was compounded by feelings of
abandonment from my mother.

My father soon remarried to a beautiful woman
11 years younger, a former Ms. Nevada. Did I mention
that I was born in America's Holy Land, Las Vegas?
My father and new stepmother, Sheilah, raised me to
the best of their ability, but I never felt like I fit in the
family—especially after they had their first son, Chris.
My father was in the television business, so we moved
around *a lot*, which involved different schools and constantly having to make new friends. All of these changes made me feel like an unwanted outcast growing up.

I truly believe that we all have a deep longing for
unconditional love and acceptance, and when that is
not being met, then we will seek it elsewhere.

During my junior year in high school, our weekends were full of mischief. We were total thugs. Two aggravated assault with deadly weapons charges later, and I could begin to see where all of this was headed. I had some friends going to jail, some killed, and another friend deported. I spent two years in criminal and civil courts working through those charges alongside my mother, Beverly. Man, did I put her through it! As the charges were wrapping up and my time in high school was coming to an end, I had some decisions to make regarding college.

With the intent of attempting to stay out of trouble, I decided on a small liberal arts Catholic College in Houston called the University of St. Thomas. Though my fighting had stopped, I began working in nightclubs around the area and selling some drugs to pay the bills. Gradually, I stopped selling drugs and began to focus more on my education. The school made me take classes on theology, which opened me up to the Bible and the things of God.

When it was time to graduate, I still didn't know what I wanted to do with my life though I was graduating with a degree in radio/TV and a minor in theology.

At the time, my father had just moved to Miami,

and it was one of the epicenters for modeling at the time in the early 2000s. In college, people had asked if I were a model, so I figured I'd give it a go and meet with some agents in Miami. The first agent I met with sent me on a "go see" with a famous photographer shooting the campaigns for Abercrombie and Fitch. I naively showed up and asked the photographer how long he'd been taking pictures, not knowing what a big deal he was. He laughed and then booked me on the spot. So, my first modeling job was for Abercrombie. I decided to move to Miami, and my father and I got an apartment together in South Beach.

Those two years were quite the experience. I went after just about everything that the films and music I grew up watching promoted. I had a sense of fame, hung around wealthy and famous people and the most beautiful women in the world, and had access to the best parties on the planet. Yet, by the end of those two years, I was more miserable than I'd ever been. I had hit rock top, which is much worse than rock bottom. At the bottom, at least you have somewhere to go!

It was a sobering reality. I felt desperate for truth as I felt like I'd taken a cultural pill of deception which left me internally sick, lonely, and angry. I knew there had to be more to life—I could feel it in my gut. In that moment, I let out a desperate cry from the depths of my soul as I prayed a fearfully dreadful prayer. I don't recall the exact words, but the essence of what I prayed was this, "God, are you real?"

Then something utterly unexplainable happened.

The Encounter

An instant thrust of electricity surged through my body, pinning my back to the cold tile floor. Electric power and love were coursing through me, leaving every hair on my body standing at attention toward their Maker. I was completely and utterly paralyzed under this otherworldly power. Tears rose from the deep and pooled into my eyes. They then began to trickle out of the corners and stream down the outside of my face as I realized I'd encountered something—SomeOne—eternal.

After what seemed like 20 minutes, it dissipated, and I regained control of my faculties and senses. I quickly grabbed my keys off the counter and raced out the door to my friend's apartment. I exuberantly wanted to share this good news with them. As I burst through their door, I began to tell them my experience, and the only language I had for what had happened was that "I had encountered eternity."

The next night, as I lay on my bed, still reeling with

wonder from the previous day's experience, I began to pray again, hoping for another experience.

That night, my hopes were realized. It may seem strange, but it was as if a massive weighty hand pressed upon my chest, causing physical paralysis once again. Yet this time, something was different. Before my very eyes, what looked like a video screen appeared above my bed. I began to have what I now know to be called an "open vision." What began to unfold before my eyes forever changed my life.

I saw a glimpse into 2,000 years ago when Jesus was going to the cross. His face was darkened by blood. He looked mangled and beaten and was carrying a massive wooden cross upon His back, moving across my sight from right to left. All of a sudden, He turned his head toward me as if He could see me watching. It was a horrific sight, yet I couldn't look away.

As His face turned toward me, His eyes lit up and flashed with a bright white light. When His eyes met mine, they were lit up with a love-infused white light that pierced the depths of my soul. In a moment, I knew that what He was going through—the punishment inflicted upon Him—He was doing it for ME! He was laying down His life for me. It all just clicked.

I knew that God was really real! It was blowing my

mind that He had done that for me, and not just me, but all of humanity. Not only did He not rat on us for what we had done wrong, but He suffered and died for us as a completely innocent man in exchange for us to experience *His* life. WOW.

All that I had been searching after as a young man—the unconditional love, the honor, the not selling out of the friends, ALL OF IT—was actually something that God had already done for me. Yet He even took it a step further. Not only did he do it for those He called friends, but He even did it for His enemies! I was undone and it caused everything in my life to radically change.

I immediately went sober and celibate. Not out of some religious duty but out of conviction to walk purely before God. My desires just changed. I was no longer longing for the things I had pursued to fill a void.

What I beheld that night in South Beach forever changed me at what felt like a cellular level. I was a new man, and I wanted to live like that man Jesus.

From that transformative encounter in South Beach, I had a fresh vision in my heart. In that moment, I had an epiphany where I realized that the most influential forces in my life growing up were the films and music that I had listened to. Gangster films and gangster rap were two of the biggest culprits. The messages that these art forms carried programmed and discipled me to become a menace to society.

All of a sudden, a thought emerged that I needed to go back into Hollywood and somehow, some way, become a light in the entertainment industry. I wanted to be in the middle of all that fought for my worship and attention for so long that I ignored the only One worthy of it.

And You Will Live

When I tell you that everything in my life changed after these encounters, I mean *everything* changed! These desires that I once had for the things of this world melted away in the heat of God's love. As I made the move from the East Coast to the West Coast, I landed in Hollywood. It was an exciting season filled with wonder about God and what the future held, but it was also a season of much trepidation and fear. Everything that I had put my identity in, like my job as a model and things I ran to like drugs, alcohol, and women... those things were gone. I was left wondering who I really was as a person.

I didn't have any friends who were on the path that I was on, so I spent a lot of time alone. I tried to attend a few churches, but they really just weirded me out, to be honest.

The initial way that I saw for me to have an impact in the entertainment industry was to get into acting. My mother had a talent agency in Houston, so she had some contacts for me in LA. One of the contacts she recommended I get in touch with was a casting director. It turned out that he actually lived on the street that I had just moved onto. Of all the streets in Los Angeles, he lived a couple of blocks from me on my street! It seemed like a divine setup!

But even then, there was a war happening for who and what I would worship. I was convinced he would cast me in some of his future films. He was on a spiritual path as well, though it was not on a path that had anything to do with Jesus.

He turned me on to a bookstore in Hollywood called the Bodhi Tree, and I began to devour every spiritual book I could get my hands on. Yet, for some reason, I didn't want to touch the Bible. This casting director's spirituality began to divert me down a spiritual path that was devoid of Jesus, yet his philosophy taught that all spiritual paths lead to Heaven. Being naive to the things of the spirit, this seemed like an equitable, fair, and loving way to look at the differing religions. After all, we were all looking for God, right?

Or so I thought.

I began reading books on New Age, Buddhism, Kaballah, Scientology, Islam, Confucius, and Daoism. I also visited places of worship for these differing ideologies.

One sunny afternoon, I received a life-altering phone call from my father. He told me that he had been diagnosed with late-stage cancer. One of his doctors told him he may have one year to live, but if he did live, they would probably have to remove his tongue, and he may lose his teeth as well. Not the kind of news that gives you the confidence you need when entering a battle like cancer.

I took a deep breath as I processed all he was telling me. I proceeded to tell him that if he needed me to be there with him, I'd drop everything and move to Dallas to be with him.

When I hung up the phone, I looked over at my table and finally decided to pick up the Bible. The book that I was so averse to reading. I opened it and flipped to a random page, roulette style. It landed open to the book of Luke, and my right thumb was pointing to a particular verse which drew my eye to it.

And he answered, "You shall love the Lord your God with all your heart and with all your soul and with all your strength and with all your mind, and your neighbor as yourself." And he said to him, "You have answered correctly; do this, and you will live." (Luke 10:27-28)

The last line hit my heart! "Do this, and you will live!" You know how sometimes in life you just have this "knowing"? Well, this was one of those moments. I knew that if we could focus on loving God, my father was going to live! I didn't know it at the time, but faith was being activated in me.

The next day, my father called and said, "I'm going to need you." I quickly responded, "I'm there." Shortly after that, I packed my bags and drove from LA to Dallas.

While looking for doctors with a more positive approach to the diagnosis and treatment, we found a doctor in Little Rock, Arkansas, named Dr Suen, pronounced "Son." Looking back, I now see that there were a lot of messages along the way to encourage us, but Dr. "Son" in Little "Rock"? I now believe prophetically that we were being set up for an encounter with the Rock of Ages!

After about six months of treatment, we were able

to return to Dallas, and his treatments became further apart. I was his full-time caretaker. It was a pretty brutal thing to watch your father decline to such a dependent state. One of the things I've come to learn is that in seasons of testing like this, our deepest struggles and issues of the past come to the surface. As my father was dealing with a physical cancer eating away at his body, I began to notice a spiritual cancer that was eating away at who I was, and I didn't know it at the time, but it was something only Jesus could heal.

FREEDOM!!

While I was in Dallas, I decided to visit a church. Back when I was living in Los Angeles, I was watching a church service on TV. The pastor on the show was a large black *man's man*! This dude, in my opinion, had cajones! I had never seen a Christian with cajones. Most of them had just seemed sterile, nice, and soft. But this guy was different. His name was TD Jakes, and I found out that he had a church in Dallas. So, one Sunday in June of 2004, I decided to go for a visit!

As I entered the sanctuary, I made my way to the back so that I could "hide." Not sure what I was hiding from, but hiding seemed like the right thing to do. The service began with worship followed by preaching from Bishop Jakes. At some point in the service, I began to notice what looked like smoke in the room. This was before people started using smoke machines in churches, but my first thought was, *Is there a smoke machine in here?*

Realizing that there was no smoke machine, I began to ask myself if I was having a flashback from my days of using hallucinogens. All of a sudden, my body began to tremble, and I started to nervously sweat. This was all too much for me to handle, so I booked out the back of the church mid-service and headed for the exit!

Fearful yet intrigued by what took place in that church, I had to return the next week to try and figure out what was happening to me. This next week, the same things began to happen. First began my observation of what looked like smoke from a smoke machine in the room. Next came the body trembling and subtle nervous sweat dribbling down the sides of my face. I wanted to leave again, but I was mesmerized by Bishop Jakes's message. He was preaching something I had never heard before: the cross of Christ and what Jesus had accomplished by bearing that cross.

It was not only revelatory to my ears, but I noticed that it was diametrically opposed to every other faith system on the planet that I had studied. Every other faith system on the planet is about you—it is up to you to make yourself righteous before God, which results in self-righteousness. Christianity was about what Jesus had done for us! Completing what we could never accomplish on our own. It was a gift offered to all of mankind, and all we had to do was receive it. There was no room for self-righteousness since it had been done for us.

As He began to articulate what God had done through the cross, I flashed back to my high-rise in South Beach a couple of years prior when I had that vision of Jesus carrying His cross. I remembered how His eyes lit up with white light and reveled in the fact that this newfound knowledge gave me the language for that experience. It was thrilling and frightening all at the same time.

What does this mean for me now? I wondered. I had believed that all paths lead to Heaven, and now that no longer seemed like a possibility. It truly seemed like Jesus was the only way. A way that I would not have chosen on my own, but looking back on my experience in South Beach, it was a way that chose me.

While I was swirling, Bishop Jakes followed his sermon with an invitation for people to come up and give their lives to Jesus. It was a seemingly natural response to such a gift from God, but I was hesitant. I had two voices battling in my mind. The first one said, "Go!" The second one said, "No!" Back and forth they went like a tennis match in my mind.

Meanwhile, Bishop Jakes took a seat on the stage and said, "We're not going anywhere, as there is one more person out there who needs to give their life to Jesus tonight." The tennis match in my mind began to pick up momentum. Time seemed to stand still, and it felt as if we waited for that "one person" for like 20 minutes. I was trembling and starting to sweat, and I had one woman to my right standing between me and the aisle. All of a sudden, unprovoked, that woman side-stepped into the aisle and took one step back, opening a lane for someone to her left to walk by! I looked at that opening as a divine invitation.

I stepped into the aisle and made my way to the front to pray with a man who led me in a tear-filled prayer to receive Jesus as not only my Savior but as my Lord, my everything. I felt so free in that moment that I wanted to shout like Mel Gibson in *Braveheart*, "FREEDOM!!"

Soon after, I prayed about my future. "God, I'm going to walk with You, but there are two places on the

Israel, and the other is Sudan." For some reason, I had
fear about both of those places as they seemed like
God-forsaken, war-torn regions. But God has a sense
of humor, doesn't he?

Go Hit on that Girl!

Not long after this experience, my father and I were
in the grocery store when he saw a pretty girl around
my age shopping there. He looked at me and said, "Go
hit on that girl!" Mind you, I was at the place where I
had not dated anyone in almost two years because of
my spiritual journey as well as being a caretaker for
my father. In the past, dating had caused a world of
pain, and I just didn't know how to do it well. So, when
he suggested I go hit on a random girl in the grocery
store, I resisted since, for one, that is not my style, and
secondly, I had decided that I was done dating the way
I had done it in the past.

I decided to take it all to the Lord in prayer. I spilled
out my heart to God and then decided to make a list of
all the attributes that I wanted in a wife. It was pretty
lengthy and specific. I took the list, folded it up, and
laid it on the floor before me as I prayed this prayer,
"Father, here are my desires for a wife, but You know

what is best for me. Nevertheless, not my will be done, but Yours."

I sent forth my requests, but in my heart, I truly surrendered them to God, figuring He knows what is best for me. I knew that I was good at messing things up, especially relationships, so I figured it was best to just trust God in this matter.

You're Going to Date Her

Not long after I made my list, I decided to get a talent agent in Dallas. My father was turning a corner in his health to the point where I felt confident leaving him alone at home. I prepared a monologue for a boutique agency in Dallas, and fortunately, I was signed on. The first job they booked me on was an industrial film (just a fancy way of saying "training video") for RadioShack. RadioShack was a huge company at the time, with stores all over the country.

Walking into the job that day, I noticed the other actors scattered around the room, sitting in various places. To my right was a blonde girl sitting on a couch with her back to me. As I walked in, she tilted her head back, and I made contact with those crystal blue eyes. When our eyes locked, I felt something like an eternal pulse beckoning me toward her! All of a sudden, a foreign thought came to my mind like a foreign emissary coming to make peace on the battlefield.

You're going to date her.

A conflict of emotions surged through my body— excitement *and* confusion. The confusion stemmed from the thought that I was done dating while the voice in my head was so strikingly clear that I thought it just might be God. The excitement came from the thought of actually dating this beauty my eyes had just fallen upon. She was stunning.

That day, we connected. I found out she was also a jazz singer and had an album about to be released. However, she also told me she sang in nightclubs, and my heart sank. The type of girls that I had known from my club days were not the type of girls I would be willing to date anymore. Still, I felt a drawing to get her number and get to know her, and I asked her if I could come to her album release party.

Halfway through our shoot, she got up to leave to head to another acting job. I have to be honest: I chickened out and didn't ask for her number, yet I had a thought that if it were meant to be, I'd run into her again. There was a bit of faith in that thought, yet it was also mixed with an excuse for my cowardice.

Fortunately for me, we had the same agency, so our

agent had sent the audition information to all the actors on a bulk email. That meant we all had each other's email addresses. This is when, in my telling of our story, I jokingly state that she stalked me and hunted me down! She vehemently denies that, but this is my story, and I'm sticking to it!

Since I had mentioned to her that I wanted to attend her album release, she pulled my email out of that bulk email and sent me the details for it. Being the smooth operator that I was, I decided not to go. I emailed her later, asking her for her number, but then waited a couple of weeks to call her. (She later told me that this drove her nuts.) The day that I finally decided to call, it just so happened to be her birthday. So, while she would tell you I was frustrating her, I had impeccable timing!

On that phone call, she mentioned that she felt some changes coming into her life but didn't quite know what they were. I had felt some changes coming in my life as well, so I suggested we go grab a bite to eat at a sushi restaurant and figure it out together.

A few minutes after I sat down at the bar in front of the sushi chefs, Meredith came walking through the door. I don't recall how our conversation started, but before she ordered food, she let me know the lay of the land and the ground rules for hanging out with her. It was as if she had a list of how she wanted to be treated. I'd never met anyone so forward. Then, she dropped the bomb on me.

There were about five things on her list, but I didn't hear anything past the second one. The first one was that she didn't get drunk. I liked that because I didn't either, so *check*! The second one was that she was a virgin. *But you're a club girl,* I thought. *Did you just say that you were a unicorn?*

As she went down her list, I was still stuck on *virgin.* This also put the fear of God in me. I had never met a girl this age who had kept herself pure for her husband.

From that moment on, I was definitely attracted to her, but I treated her with kid gloves. I kept my heart at a distance, which I knew confused her, but I didn't want to go deep with her if I didn't think it was going to last. She was too precious for me to play with her emotions if I were not all the way serious.

We dated a whole four months before we got engaged, and then we were married three months later. We barely knew each other at all, yet we both had a massive passion for Jesus, acting, and impacting the world for God. She even laughed at my jokes!

Lay Down Your Life

A month before we got engaged, we had gone to my mother's home in South Texas for Thanksgiving. On the way home, we had decided to fast that day to seek God about some important decisions regarding the future. One of them was how our relationship was to move forward, and the other was if I should move back to Los Angeles. The kicker was that I needed a place to live for a season while I looked for a more permanent place to rent.

As we drove back into Dallas, we pulled into a parking lot near SMU. As we sat there talking, I received a call from the owner of a commercial agency in LA that represented all the biggest actors on the planet. We had become friends when I waited tables at that sushi restaurant. We hadn't talked in months, but for "some reason," he decided to call that day. He called to ask if I was going to move back to LA because he was doing some work on his home and needed someone to stay there and look after it!

You can't make this stuff up. We both knew that I had to move back to LA, but that left a huge question regarding our relationship. Earlier that day, we were listening to a sermon where the Pastor said he waited 5 years before asking his wife to marry him. So I looked at Meredith and said, "Would you wait 5 years for me?"

She said, "Nope. If you can't make up your mind then move on!" I was so drawn to her clarity and boldness. In that moment I decided that I was going to ask her to marry me on my birthday which was the following month, so when she said "yes," we would both be moving to LA together.

Within a week of being in LA, I ran into an old acquaintance at the gym, and he had an opening at his four-plex next to Paramount Studios. It was perfect and in our price range, so we signed a lease immediately.

Meredith and I both got top acting coaches in LA. My classes were more focused on dramatic acting, and her classes were on sitcom acting. She was doing so well that her coach was telling our manager that she would book a sitcom pilot in the next coming pilot season. Her coach was the onset acting coach for the TV show *Friends*—she was a big deal!

In addition to work, I had some friends who ran a ministry called Models for Christ. They turned us on to a little church in the ghetto of Gardena, a suburb of LA about 45 minutes from our home. It was a small, peculiar group of people consisting of mostly homeless folks, a few people from the neighborhood, and one well-to-do white couple that would bring their kid's friends from USC. The pastor was from South Africa, and he preached six days a week. I was so hungry for the Word of God that I'd drive there almost every day!

This pastor preached a pretty basic but radical message. The core of his message was something like this: "It is not YOUR life. Lay down your life! Give it fully over to God, every part of it. The most responsible thing you can do is surrender your life, your dreams, *everything* to God and let Him take over!"

After a couple of months of hearing this message, we felt compelled to lay down our lives—even our dreams in the entertainment industry. Around this time, I first learned of an organization called Youth with a Mission, better known as YWAM. They had schools all over the world, but I saw that they had one in Jerusalem. That blew me away! The thought of learning more about the Bible in the place where Jesus walked sucked me in. I was sold!

I talked to Meredith about it and decided to send them an inquiry about their program. That night, we prayed an audacious prayer. It went something like this, "Lord, if you want us to go on this 6-month program to Israel, you need to take care of our apartment and all of its bills, pay for us to go there, and take care of my job and all of my new clients."

No big deal, right?

And wouldn't you know it, He answered every single thing down to the detail.

It's all About Worship

Before we moved to Israel, while lying in bed one morning, I awoke to a thunderous revelation that my wife mentioned in the previous chapter. I not only startled my wife, but I startled myself. I woke the both of us up screaming, "IT'S ALL ABOUT WORSHIP!"

"What is?" Mer asked.

"Everything!"

The thing is, I had no cognitive understanding of what I was saying. It was like I had been impregnated with something so deep in my spirit that I knew beyond a shadow of a doubt that it was *truth*. It was a deeply spiritual experience that was literally beyond my own comprehension. Next to getting saved, it was the deepest truth I had ever encountered.

Yet, at that point in time, I was still in my first year of becoming a Christian and knew very little about worship. I actually had no idea why Christians even sang songs in church. But after that, I knew that the ultimate battle was over who or what was going to be worshipped. That moment did something so profound in my spirit that my mind is *still* catching up to it.

And our time in Israel began the process of unveiling this truth in ways that I was simply unprepared for.

3

UNLEASHING ANGELS

Meredith

66 I TRAINED YOU IN the world, and I will use it all."

One day during our mission trip in Turkey, I was apologizing to the Lord for all the worldly singing, performance, and acting. And what He told me was striking: "I trained you in the world, and I will use it all."

Before that moment, He hadn't asked me to give it up. But now, He knew that I would need to lay it down because the business *definitely* had a hold of me, not Him.

His timing was perfect. It was a sacrifice much like Abraham laying down Isaac—I didn't know how it was going to play out, but I knew I had to be obedient. After a lot of kicking, screaming, and full-blown temper tantrums, I finally did it. I laid all my plans and dreams on the altar, and He changed everything in a single moment. I was saved as a kid, but I truly felt like a new creation after that moment of surrender.

After we completed the last week of our mission in Turkey, we headed back to the West Bank of Israel for a few more weeks before our school was set to end. As part of our schooling, we were in a small group of about six people that met once a week. Each week, we would all pray over someone specific, and this particular week, it was my turn. My request was simple: "All I have ever known is performance. I want to know what it looks like to worship. Please pray for me!"

I sat in the cold, hard metal chair in the middle of the circle with my hands out, ready to receive. The hodge-podge group from different countries huddled around me and began to pray. One of the girls in our group was a young, blonde-haired girl named Janell. She had been a missionary in Thailand before she had come to YWAM with us in Israel. I had always been impressed with the way she lived—first of all, she was YOUNG! Second, she would fast for breakthrough for the people around her, and I had never met someone who contended for others the way she did.

Well, that girl put her hand on my back and prayed with incredible authority:

"Lord, I pray you show Meredith what it looks like when she worships you, and I pray that you show her right *now!*"

The Lord answered that prayer on the spot, and what took place altered the course of our lives forever.

Michael

You Need to Sing!

Once a week in Jerusalem, we would meet with a small group to connect and pray together. The meeting place was in an old Baptist compound near the Garden Tomb just outside the ancient walls of the Old City in Jerusalem. Each week, we would single someone out for the entire group to pray over. This particular week, it was Meredith's turn.

She shared about how she had been struggling to make the internal shift in her heart from performance to worship, and that was the area she wanted us to direct our prayers toward. So, we all gathered around in a circle, laying our hands on her. As we began to pray, a girl named Janell—a powerful prayer warrior who helped prostitutes get off the streets in Thailand—prayed in a way I had never heard before. She actually prayed in a way that offended my new believer sensibilities. She prayed, "Lord, would you show Meredith what happens in the spiritual realm when she worships You, *and show her right now!*"

It was the last part of the phrase that offended me because I immediately thought, *You can't tell God what to do!*

However, revelation came bursting through my line of offense! Even though Janell prayed for the Lord to show Meredith, He showed *me* instead. Maybe because she and I are one, or for some greater purpose I don't understand, but in a moment, it was as if my spiritual eyes—the eyes of my heart—were opened to see into eternity! I know this sounds crazy, but in the blink of an eye, I saw an entire host of angels.

In that sliver of time, I understood what they were thinking, I could feel what they were feeling, and I knew what they were created to do. Some of them were created for war, some for healing, ministering, and deliverance. I could feel this pent-up holy frustration emanating from within them as they waited in holy anticipation for Meredith to worship. It was as if every fiber of their being was screaming for Meredith to sing to the Lord. And I knew it was because when she sang to the Lord, they were released into the earth to do what they were created to do. They wanted her to sing to the Lord as if life itself depended on it! In fact, I could literally feel their internal scream.

That burden, along with the rest of that revelation, completely short-circuited me to the point that I fell to the ground ugly crying for what seemed like 20 minutes. What I realized in that moment is that in the eternal realm, normal ways of communication are not necessary. All the information about you is just available for others to access, including one's thoughts and feelings.

While I was lying there crying like a baby, our small group, which included my brother, Chris, was looking at me, wondering what in the world was going on. They had never seen me act like that and quickly asked me if I was okay. I just nodded my head in affirmation with a thumbs up, still sobbing, unable to get out any words. Once I could shake the emotion of it all, I looked at my wife with the passion of Heaven's angels in my eyes and said, "You need to sing!"

"What do you mean? Like, now?" She responded.

I figured that I owed her a little explanation of what just happened, so I filled her in. It was such a holy moment for me, I didn't really tell many people about it for almost a year. Since I had studied other religions, I wanted to make sure my experience was biblical since I had no frame of reference for what I had just experienced. I wanted everything in my life to line up with the Bible. In my mind, I wanted no room for deception. I'd lived my entire life in deception, so I strongly felt I needed to guard the truth at all costs.

But that wasn't all that came from that encounter. I also knew that we were supposed to move back to Dallas, and that the Lord was going to provide a recording studio for Meredith to record her songs. I can't tell you exactly why or how, only that I simply knew it was supposed to happen!

We had been wrestling with what we were going to do after YWAM, and had been thinking of moving to the West Bank, where I would teach English to the Palestinians. Yet in that moment, it was oddly clear in my heart what we were supposed to do. I told Meredith, and she was in agreement with that decision.

It was time to move back to Dallas.

Releasing Angels

We moved back to Dallas with major expectation that God was up to something. The first week back, we didn't tell anyone that we were back, as we wanted to just spend that week in prayer, seeking the Lord for direction. Within that time, a music producer in Dallas named Aaron Kelley had heard that Meredith was back in town. He reached out to her and said, "I heard you are back in Dallas. I've been waiting for two years for you to move back! If you have any music you'd like to work on, I'd love to open my studio and services to you free of charge. I just believe in you!"

I was crazy to see our prayers being manifested before our eyes—not to mention in such a short time! I knew in my heart that God called us back to Dallas for her to do an album, and within a week of us being home, not seeking out a studio or a producer, *wham*! God sends us one.

They spent the next few months working on the album. When they first began, I told Meredith that she should include a song about the encounter in Jerusalem and center the theme of the album around releasing angels. Well, I guess she forgot that conversation because about a month later, she came up to me and said she had a great idea for a song called "Releasing Angels." I gave her an odd look but still said, "That's a great idea!"

Is This Even in the Bible?!

While Meredith was walking out her side of the releasing angels experience, I was walking out my side in a different way. I was on a mission to figure out what it all meant. There was a deep need to understand what I had experienced and find others who may have had similar experiences, as I was somewhat skeptical of what had just happened to me.

While searching online, I came across a book called *Open My Eyes, Lord* by a Baptist pastor named Gary Oates. It was about a man who had his spiritual eyes opened in such a way that he was able to see into the spiritual realm. The book looked pretty provocative, so I ordered it.

When it arrived, I opened the package and took the book out to set it on the counter. As I was looking at the book, my phone rang. It was a friend of my father named Steve Kirk, or as we called him, Kirky. Kirky was an old Willie Nelson roadie outlaw. To say he was a character is an understatement! His parents were old revivalists, so he had a genuine hunger for the things of God. He began to tell me a story of how his assistants went down to a conference in Houston to hear a man speak named—you guessed it—Gary Oates!

"Have you heard of him?" he said.

My heart stopped. Here I was, staring at this random book I had just ordered, and he was asking me if I'd heard of the author. I could almost hear God audibly etching my heart, "You are on the right track, Michael. Pay attention!"

Needless to say, I dove into that book that afternoon. The essence of Gary's story is that he was a Baptist pastor on the verge of burnout when he decided to go on one last missions trip to Brazil. While he was down there, he met a man who allegedly was able to see into the spirit realm. So, Gary asked that man to pray for his spiritual eyes to be opened. The man prayed for Gary in Portuguese, but according to Gary, he didn't feel anything, nor was he able to understand the prayer. He simply moved on with the day.

Later that night, they were in a worship service together. The man who prayed for Gary was playing drums, and at one point, he started into a war-like rhythm. All of a sudden, Gary began to see angels fly into the room! They flew over people in the congregation with swords and began to cut dark clouds of oppression off of their heads.

I was speechless. This was the essence of what I had seen in my vision in Israel: Angels being released at the sound of worship!

But is this dynamic even in the Bible?

From there, I really began to dive into the Scriptures. One of the first stories I recall coming across was the story of Jehoshaphat in 2 Chronicles 20. Jehoshaphat was the leader of Israel, and he found himself with a multitude of enemies coming after him. He was surrounded and greatly afraid, so he began to seek God with some of the other leaders of Israel and Judah. As they were seeking God, the Spirit of the Lord came upon a Levite named Jahaziel, and he began to prophesy to them, saying:

> *Thus says the LORD to you, "Do not be afraid and do not be dismayed at this great horde, for the battle is not yours but God's..."* (2 Chronicles 20:15)

> *"You will not need to fight in this battle. Stand firm, hold your position, and see the salvation of the LORD on your behalf, O Judah and Jerusalem." Do not be afraid and do not be dismayed. Tomorrow go out against them, and the LORD will be with you.* (verse 17)

> *And when he had taken council with the people, he appointed those who were to sing to the LORD and praise him in holy attire, as they went before the army, and say, "Give thanks to the LORD,*

for his steadfast love endures forever." And when
they began to sing and praise, the LORD set an
ambush against the men of Ammon, Moab, and
Mount Seir, who had come against Judah, so that
they were routed. (verses 21-22)

This is an unbelievable story, right? They didn't war like we would think they would go to war. They sent the band into the battlefield to sing songs of thanksgiving and praise! Yet, look at what God did when they praised Him! The enemies were confused, and they won the battle.

So, did God release angels into the battle? The text doesn't explicitly say that, but most scholars believe that it is inferred from the text.

The next set of Scriptures I came across that seemed to illustrate this reality were in 1 Samuel 16. King Saul was tormented by a spirit, which some could associate with depression. Some of the men in the king's service had an idea to bring in a young man named David, who was skilled in playing the harp. They believed that the Lord was with him.

1 Samuel 16:23 states "And whenever the harmful spirit from God was upon Saul, David took the lyre and played it with his hand. So Saul was refreshed and was well, and the harmful spirit departed from him."

Isn't that interesting? What was it about David playing that caused the harmful spirit to depart? Were angels released into the room like Gary Oates had seen in Brazil?

The third text that really lit me up was in the New Testament book of Acts 16. It details the journey of Paul and Silas as they were on mission preaching the gospel. As they came to Macedonia, they cast a demon out of a fortune teller. This set the city in an uproar, and the city leaders drug Paul and Silas through the streets, stripped them of their clothes, and had them beaten with rods! If that weren't enough, the city leaders threw them into prison and fastened their feet into stocks.

I don't know about you, but this is not what someone bargains for when trying to follow God and help people! Reading this story for the first time, I remember putting myself into their shoes and thinking about how I'd react in their situation. For one, I know I'd be complaining to God, wondering where He was. I'd be salty!

Yet Paul and Silas were on a different playing field and knew something that I had not learned just yet.

About midnight Paul and Silas were praying and singing hymns to God, and the prisoners were listening to them, and suddenly there was a great earthquake, so that the foundations of the prison were shaken. And immediately all the doors were opened, and everyone's bonds were unfastened. (Acts 16:25-26)

Again, something extraordinary was happening in the midst of worship. After reading this passage for the first time, I was left wondering how they knew to do this, as their reaction was anything but normal. Again, their response was certainly not the one I would have had in that situation! Still, I knew the Lord was meeting me through His Word and that I would continue to get clarity through it.

Reading these ancient stories, I was awestruck with wonder. God was confirming that my experience in Jerusalem was not only legitimate, but it was biblical! It was as if the veil between Heaven and Earth was being pulled back, and God was revealing that He wanted to fight my battles for me *and* with me.

For so much of my life, I had fought alone. I had fought *my* way—the *world's* way—but I was no longer a part of the world. Would God really fight for us all this way and send His angels to assist us on Earth? I still had so many unanswered questions, but faith was stirring in me that God would provide the answers as I needed them.

Back in Jerusalem, right before we moved back to Dallas, I had seen another vision of Meredith in worship, singing to God. In this particular vision, when she sang, I could see sound waves going toward the Heavens. Those sound waves became an interstellar highway of sorts for the angels to ride upon and come into the earth realm. It was a fascinating sight to see for sure, but my initial thought after I saw this vision was, again, *Is this even biblical?*

At this point, I wasn't even familiar with the story of Jacob's ladder, which this vision could be associated with. You might have even thought about that as you read! However, I had no idea, and I was curious to know if there was any validity to what I was seeing or if it was just my imagination. In time, I came across an obscure Scripture that seemed to validate the vision.

In the Old Testament (OT), the sacrifices to God were mostly animal sacrifices, as well as bringing in part of the harvest to the temple. In the New Testament (NT), sacrifices shift to thanksgiving, praise, and almsgiving. Even in these two examples, we see that the OT is a shadow of what is in the NT! Now, hold that thought. We'll come back to it.

In Judges 13, there is a story of an angel who comes

to visit the parents of Sampson. Manoah, Sampson's father, offers to feed it, not realizing it was an angel. This is where it gets interesting.

> And the angel of the LORD said to Manoah, "If you detain me, I will not eat of your food. But if you prepare a burnt offering, then offer it to the LORD." (For Manoah did not know that he was the angel of the LORD.) (Judges 13:16)

So Manoah took the young goat with the grain offering, and offered it on the rock to the LORD, to the one who works wonders, and Manoah and his wife were watching. And when the flame went up toward heaven from the altar, the angel of the LORD went up in the flame of the altar. Now Manoah and his wife were watching, and they fell on their faces to the ground. (Verses 19-20)

Did you catch that? The angel rode the flame *back* to Heaven! Somehow, the angel *needed* that sacrifice. Remember, the Old Testament sacrifices were a foreshadowing of what would come in the NT. Could our sacrifice of praise and worship somehow be that same pathway for the angels, just like Jacob's ladder?

These texts again confirmed to me that I was definitely on the right course. I was seeing that God fights for us when we worship, people come out of their prisons and captivity, and angels are even released when we offer up a sacrifice of praise! Not only that, but there was more talk about worship and praise in the Bible than I had realized. Yet, it also left me with a lot of questions.

What exactly *is* worship? *Why* is worship so powerful? How do we worship? Is worship only through song and instruments?

So, we'll endeavor to get into those questions together. We now know that there is a war for who and what will be worshipped, that there is power when we worship, and that all of life is about worship. Let's dig a little a deeper in the next chapter into what Scripture tells us worship is all about.

4

THE POWER OF WORSHIP

UNDOUBTEDLY, ONE OF the most influential pop stars of the 20th century was Michael Jackson, a singer/songwriter known as the "King of Pop." Toward the end of his life there were some serious allegations regarding his character; however, that is not the focus I'd like for us to take here. Michael was a fascinating character with worldwide influence, fame, and untold wealth. He could literally have anything he wanted in life.

He was born a man with dark skin and curly hair. By the end of his life, he had white skin and straight hair, and his face had been completely transformed through reconstructive surgery. Have you ever considered what or who he was transforming himself into? Some have said that he was just an eccentric artist or that he wanted to be a white man, but if you look a bit deeper, there was definitely something else going on.

Canadian Philosopher, Marshall McLuhan, known for his work on media theory, famously said, "We become what we behold"—a phrase that has been made common in worship circles though it was first coined in the context of media. What he's saying is that what we behold with our eyes, ears, and affections are so powerful that within the beholding there is actually the power to become like what we see. That was—and still is—my story. What I saw became an anchor into the future. It was pulling me into a destination that had the appearance of life, but its end was pain and destruction. Yet, when I "saw" the Lord, He became my anchor of hope, leading me to an alternate future filled with promise and love!

Think about this concept for a moment as it pertains to your own life. Do you remember having a childhood idol? A hero when you were growing up? Maybe it was a pro sports player or a Disney princess. Have you ever thought about the fact that most of us played dress up, wanting to be like them so badly that we mimicked what they looked like? What about the power of film, social media, or magazines provoking us to compare ourselves to what other people look like and idolize their lives?

Considering the life of Michael Jackson, it was obvious that there was almost a cult following of his personal worshippers who would fawn and faint over him at his performances. However, if you consider his life personally, it becomes obvious that he had an object of worship in his own life—so much so that he completely changed the way he looked.

Let's take that a little deeper, shall we? What was the name of his ranch? Neverland Ranch. Who did he keep company with that was so controversial? Little kids. It should be obvious by now that I'm talking about Peter Pan. Yes, I'm saying that Michael Jackson was turning himself into Peter Pan.

If you need further proof, look at the face of Peter Pan and then look at Michael Jackson later in life. It's shockingly similar! He was literally transforming himself into Peter Pan.

Now, that may be an extreme example, but it speaks clearly to the statement that we become what we behold. And *that* is the essence of worship. We were created to behold someone and become like them, and that someone is *Him*. God designed us to become one with the object of our complete affections. That's why the first of the Ten Commandments is this: "You shall have no other gods before me." Firsts are important to God, and so is what and who we worship! Life begins with God and His love for us, so when we return it back to Him, the foundation of our lives begin with that intimate union with Him.

Why is Our Worship Significant?

Up to this point, we've discussed the power of worship, the battle of who is going to be worshipped, and pulled back the veil a bit to see what takes place in the spiritual realm when we worship. So, what exactly is worship, anyways? I've rarely heard it defined, and maybe you share the same sentiments!

Around 2008, I heard a sermon online where the speaker quoted the Archbishop of Canterbury, William Temple, who defines worship like this: "Worship is the submission of all of my nature to God. It is the quickening of consciousness by His holiness, nourishment of mind by His truth, purifying of imagination by His beauty, opening of the heart to His love, and submission of will to His purpose. All this gathered up in adoration is the greatest expression of which we are capable."

That last part deserves another read, right? "All of this gathered up in adoration is the greatest expression of which we are capable!"

I *love* this definition. But why is this the greatest expression? Does God need our worship? If He's God, clearly He doesn't *need* our worship. I once heard an atheist try to make the argument that God must be some egomaniac who demands our worship because He's so insecure that He "needs" it.

Let's be honest here. God, who has existed before we ever came to be, does not need a single thing outside of Himself to exist. He's the all-sufficient One, the Great I Am. He just *is*! In fact, Acts 17:24-25 states, "The God who made the world and everything in it, being Lord of heaven and earth, does not live in temples made by man, nor is he served by human hands, as though he needed anything, since he himself gives to all mankind life and breath and everything."

He's expressed His love to us by denying Himself and laying down His life for us. He didn't demand or ask for us to worship Him out of His need. In fact, it was quite the opposite. But this still begs the question: Why is our worship so significant to Him?

Let's explore that biblically together.

From beginning to end, the Bible speaks of people who worship in a personal expression as well as a corporate expression. Both are significant, as *what* we worship becomes our true north. The problem is, God's people aren't always worshipping *Him*! The biblical narrative shows that everything seems to be vying for the affections of the people of God—from golden calves to Asherah poles, temple prostitutes to Baal, to a multitude of gods. Throughout the OT, Jewish people constantly jostle between monotheism (the belief that there is only one true God) and the temptation to polytheism (the belief that there is more than one god).

In the book of Exodus, when Moses went to Pharaoh to liberate the Jewish people from slavery, he said to Pharaoh, "Let my people go, that they may worship!" (Exodus 8:1 NIV) Have you ever wondered why God wanted to liberate His people *unto* worship?

As I quoted earlier, "You become what you behold." In the same way that I wanted to be a gangster as a kid because of what I was beholding, I believe that God wanted His people to come out into the wilderness to worship Him so they could be reminded who they were as sons and daughters of God! They had been slaves for 400 years, so their identity was skewed. How they valued themselves was skewed. How they saw the world was skewed. God wanted to renew their minds and liberate them unto *Himself* so they were no longer bound by their slavery mindset but freed to rule and reign as sons and daughters loved by the living God.

I'm telling you, when you start to think about it, you'll find that it really is all about worship!

Continuing to dive into why worship is so significant to God, let's fast forward to when Jesus was being tempted with all the kingdoms of the world. In Luke 4:6-8, the devil tells Jesus, "'To you I will give all this authority and their glory, for it has been delivered to me, and I give it to whom I will. If you, then, **will worship me**, it will all be yours.' And Jesus answered him, 'It is written, **"You shall worship the Lord your God, and him only shall you serve."'"**

The word for "worship" in that verse is *proskynéō,* and the word for "serve" is *latreuo.* We'll come back to that in a minute.

Alright. So, what we see in those verses in Luke 4 is that all of history was contingent upon a potential act of worship. Not only that, but *who* was going to be worshipped. The devil clearly knows the power of worship, what's at stake with worship, and what's exchanged in worship. Think about what would have happened if Jesus had fallen for satan's ploy! Clearly, Jesus's destiny was to have all the kingdoms of the world, and the devil knew it. Yet the devil was in "let's make a deal" mode, offering Jesus an easier route to His destiny without having to die to Himself on that silly old cross.

Make no mistake about it, the devil is still offering that same deal to all of us.

I think it's important to notice the order of words Jesus used in response to the devil. He said to first worship the Lord, and then to serve! He stresses the "becoming," which is a result of worship. What's implied from that is we will then emerge into the "doing." There is a ploy for the devil to turn us into "human *doings*" before we are "human *beings*."

Think about the story of Mary and Martha. Mary chose the greater thing, which was to sit at the feet of Jesus, and Martha got rebuked for worrying about so much. (see Luke 10:41) That worrying caused her to strive and work before she'd spent any time with Jesus. God is the great I Am, not the great I *do*! As we behold Him in worship, our God-given identity is revealed and, thus, our calling!

As we fast forward to the last book of the Bible, in Revelation 5, we get the clearest picture of what the throne room of God looks like in Heaven. In Heaven, the people are playing stringed instruments, singing new songs, and praying along with the angels! It's interesting and important to note that those closest to God in Heaven—those in the throne room—are *worshipping.*

Now, I hear people say all the time, "But Michael, the work we do for the Lord is our worship!" To that, I absolutely agree... to a degree. One of the Hebrew words for worship is *avad,* which is the word used in Exodus 8:1 mentioned above. "Let my people go that they may **worship**," which some translations translate as *serve.*

Part of the understanding of the definition for *avad* is that your work is your worship—to truly serve. The Greek word for this is *latrueo,* which I noted above, referenced in Luke 4. It's true that the vocation the Lord has called us to is indeed avad/latreuo worship unto Him. However, I would argue that the Lord could have chosen any vocation to be displayed before His throne in worship. He could have had accountants working on numbers, bakers making cookies, auto mechanics working on heavenly spacecrafts, yet He chose to display musicians and singers. This begs the question, why?

The Bible doesn't specifically give us the answer, so we have to make some inferences. First of all, He must like it when we sing! I mean, God stresses the importance of unity in the Spirit, as stated in Ephesians 4:3. What unifies a group of people more than music? In a given moment, we can all be singing the same song with the same lyrics and melodies, feeling the same feelings, totally in agreement with one another.

Musicologist Bjorn Vickhoff of the Sahlgrenska Academy in Sweden did a study with a group of high school students singing a hymn that said, "God is love, let heav'n adore him. God is love, let earth rejoice…" What he noticed blew his mind. They were wearing heart rate monitors while singing, and he noticed a slowing of their heart rates, which is awesome in and of itself. However, what really struck him was that almost immediately, the singers' heart rates became synchronized.[1]

Even science agrees that singing together unifies us! Music also has a way of bypassing our minds and getting right to the heart. Think about what it looks like when a person bows in worship with their head to the ground. In that posture, their head is below their heart! God is after our hearts, and music has a way of connecting us at a heart level like nothing else. Songs help us to behold an invisible God with the eyes of our hearts!

Did you know that the largest book of the Bible in terms of number of pages is the book of Psalms, which is a book of *songs*? Hopefully, I'm clearly making the point that musical worship is important to God. It's also important to the devil, and important to humanity. This is why we must understand its significance in our own lives.

There are two Hebrew words and two Greek words that are defined as worship in the Bible. In each language, one of them is defined as "service," and the other word is defined as "bowing down in reverence and/or adoration." The Greek word for worship, *proskyneo*, goes a bit further with the imagery, and it means to fall prostrate and bow with one's head to the ground and it also means to "kiss, like a dog licking its master's hand," according to Strong's Concordance.

Side note: Haven't you noticed how people start to kinda look like their dogs? Kinda strange, right?

Okay, moving right along. Regardless of whether that dog reference freaks you out or not, the bottom line is that worship is an act of *love* in response to the awe and wonder of Almighty God. That response can look like singing, but it also can look like bowing in reverence, jubilant joy expressed in dance, crying in awe, or even starting a new job in obedience to what God is asking you to do. (see Ephesians 3:14, 2 Samuel 6:14-16, Hebrews 5:7)

The Greatest Expression of Worship

So, why is all of this so important to God? Well, intimate connection is at the core of worship. It's not just expression for expression's sake, it's a heart connection with Love Himself. God is seeking us out, and worship is what connects us at the most intimate level.

After the fall of mankind, sin entered in, and we became self-aware or self-centered (Genesis 3:7). It has been said that sin is a man turned in on himself. This is why a lot of people do drugs because often, we are not comfortable in our skin as a result of shame. Drugs help liberate us from ourselves, but they come with handcuffs. They are a counterfeit way to true freedom.

But worship is part of the antidote to the sinful nature! It gets our awareness off of us and back upon God, which is the way it was back in the garden. God wants us restored to union with Him, and that is our highest calling and position. What Jesus accomplished on

the cross dealt with the sin or chasm that separated us.
Worship provides the way back home.

At the beginning of this chapter, I asked the question following the Archbishop's' definition: Why is worship the greatest expression of which we are capable? That's a strong statement. But I think what he was getting at was that this expression is the greatest because God is, quite literally, the highest and greatest Being, and we are responding to His presence. If God is the highest, what is higher than the highest? And if we adore Him and become like the One we are adoring, and our calling emerges from that place, then what is higher or greater than that?

Nothing!

5

I MISSED JESUS!

Meredith

JOLTED AWAKE FROM that lucid in-between state of sleep, I shot up in bed with a thundering phrase running through my head: "I have missed Jesus"!

How? What?!

It was almost as if Jesus Himself was standing at the end of my bed for a split second. It felt like one of those horrible moments where you forgot something terribly important, like picking up your kid from school or showing up for an exam that you forgot to study for. But this was worse—I had forgotten JESUS!

It didn't feel like He was mad or upset; He just showed up for a split second, and my response was frantic, knowing that I had forgotten Him. I sat there with my heart pounding, bewildered as I began to fully wake up from my groggy, shaken state. I frantically tried to understand what the phrase meant.

How have I forgotten Jesus? I've literally been at a church conference for the last three days serving on the worship team. How did I miss Him?!

Now, maybe if this was a one-time occurrence, I could chalk it up to a random pizza dream. However, this continued to happen for months. I was haunted by the thought that I was doing something wrong.

Today, looking back at those times around 2009-2010, I realize what I was taking as admonishment was actually a beautiful invitation. As I'm sitting here writing, thankful tears are actually running down my face as I remember that season.

So, what was it? How was I forgetting Him? Let me take it back for a moment.

As young believers, excited and zealous to change the world, our assumption was that God would just open up our ministry. We were holding onto a few radical encounters and had a new purpose to "release angels through worship." It was a straight line to what we were called to, right? Michael and I were gonna hit the big stage and start to testify.

Of course, that was simply our assumption at the time. We saw, from our extremely limited viewpoint, the end goal, and we wanted to get there as soon as possible! Thankfully, the Lord always knows the better way. The straight line to our calling often ends up taking hard left turns, sometimes going in the opposite direction of the way we think. Oh, but He knows that the twists and turns are actually the exact training we need—even though that can be near impossible to see in the moment.

Alright, let's go back to the forgetting Jesus. Right after YWAM in Israel, we were excited to worship, full of revelation and ready to pour out our overflowing hearts. What the Lord had deposited in our spirits wasn't a conscious understanding that we could spell out just yet, but there was a fire and hunger to go fully after Him. In that pursuit, we ended up at a passionate church that was truly a pioneer in the prophetic. Their church contended for high-level prophetic words, and we were excited to learn more.

When we were together, it was time to war and declare what the Lord was saying on the earth. We would sing about what we would do for God, taking what He was saying and declaring it into the earth. We had so many profound times when we would see things in the news reflect what God had just shown us in prayer days or even weeks before. This church loved to pray and prophesy, and God was showing them global events before they ever happened! We were elated to be there. However, what I didn't understand in my immaturity was that this church expected that you were cultivating intimate times of prayer and worship on your own.

I gained some incredible things from that season. I learned to sing spontaneously and prophetically, watching people get whole songs with revelation and rhyme. It was unreal! I like to joke that I got training with the special forces of the prophetic. However, as a worshipper, I eventually felt tired and dry. I couldn't understand why because I was prophesying and singing so often. It got to the point where I started to feel like I couldn't even worship any longer, and I began to question if God had even led us there. Plus, all my dreams about missing Jesus!

Now, I'm not blaming the church for what I was feeling, as they were walking out what they felt called to do. This all had to do with His training for me as a worshipper. Still, I was distraught. How was I missing Jesus?! But Proverbs 25:2 says, "It's the glory of God to conceal a thing: but it's the honor of kings to search out a matter."

Here's a key for you in your own life: If the Lord places a burning desire in you for something that leaves you with more questions than answers, get ready for the Lord to take you on a journey of discovery. The answers are not always easy, but the journey becomes precious history with the Lord. I've found that often the discovery process is more important than even the answers themselves.

Through a series of prophetic words and following "the river of God," the Lord moved us from Dallas to Houston. I had been hearing Houston everywhere, and though I had never thought of moving there, it felt as if we were supposed to. I honestly didn't even know what we would do there! Still, I told Michael I thought God was telling us to move.

Michael, on the other hand, wasn't so sure I was hearing from God! Especially because he had said, "I will never move back to Houston." Well, we have now learned never to say the word "never" because that most likely means you are headed in that direction!

Soon after we started talking about it, the leader at the church we were attending prophesied, "Follow the river of God that is moving at your front door."

That day, when we got home from church, a fire hydrant burst and flooded the entire street. There was a literal rushing river flowing in front of our house! You may think that's silly, but it definitely spoke to us. Our house sold within days of being listed—even in the midst of the 2008 housing market crash—so we headed to Houston shortly after. Our church blessed us into our next season, and we were off on a new adventure.

Although it felt like a two-year detour while we were in it, God had significant plans for us in Houston. For one, Michael's mom and stepdad gave their lives to Jesus, and we had the privilege of baptizing them! Then, droves of Michael's friends from his B.C. days who wouldn't step into a church started coming to our home Bible study. God showed up in powerful ways, and many in the group got saved, delivered, and set up on a path to follow Jesus! I led worship at a local church there and met some of our best friends to this day. We also had two of our kids there!

Through all this, I would still periodically have my recurring dream that I missed Jesus, but my heart was coming alive again. However, I knew there was more.

Two years into moving, we knew our season in Houston was ending. The house we were renting was being sold, and we talked about moving again. This time, it was back to Dallas.

At the time, UPPERROOM had started meeting on Sunday nights and a few days a week for prayer in Dallas. Before we left for Houston, we had been meeting with Michael and Lorisa Miller in their apartment to talk about what the Lord wanted to do in Dallas. At the end of our chapter in Houston, we both knew we wanted to be around these friends because they were passionately pursuing the Lord.

Going All In

I'll never forget the day I first walked up the old steps to a room above a vet clinic and entered through the doors to a UPPERROOM service (if you could call it that). There were maybe 50 people there that evening, but I felt something fresh and alive in my spirit. And it was definitely not the room! There were brown stains all over the carpet and rickety chairs lined up by an old makeshift stage. It was anything but fresh.

Though I was not about to let my baby crawl on that stained floor, I knew there was something incredibly sweet happening. It was clear that I was walking into something the Lord was doing, but I wasn't quite sure what it was. I also knew that I could ask to be on the worship team and get going on the team immediately, but I really felt the Lord just wanted me to sit and listen and catch what He was doing there.

So, I did. For the first month or two, I sat in during worship and just soaked it all in. Believe it or not, it was *not* the culture that you walk into today. No one sang spontaneously, and there was definitely no dancing or flags! In fact, I remember there were multiple times in the early days where Lorisa had to get up and coax people to even worship. It's funny to say that now, knowing what the culture is like these days. Still, I had such anticipation in my spirit. It was as if I'd walked right into the center of where God wanted to be. There was a hunger in the room even though we didn't outwardly express it yet.

The worship leader who was over the prayer room and worship at that time was feeling a call to move to another city, so we started meeting with the Millers once a week to pray about how we were supposed to run together. Long story short, my husband was eventually offered the position overseeing worship and prayer at UPPERROOM.

And this is where it got challenging: We had arrived in Dallas on faith and a prayer (a lot more than one, I might add). We had no jobs and two tiny kids. God pretty miraculously helped us buy a house, which is a story for another time, but we had a mortgage and needed to eat, so a job was necessary! The same week that Michael was offered the worship position for $1,000 a month, he was also offered a sales job elsewhere for six figures plus commission. Michael wrestled with that as he wanted to provide for us. In the natural, $1,000 a month wouldn't pay the bills. But I knew we were supposed to "go all in" with UPPERROOM. So, he turned down the sales job, and we jumped in headfirst!

What made this job extra interesting is that Michael doesn't sing or play an instrument. Michael only makes a joyful noise! However, because of the vision he received in Israel, worship was what he burned for. All he wanted to do was empower worshipers to worship! Also, when you are a tiny church (that didn't even want to call themselves church at the time), you get those 2-for-1 specials when you hire a couple. I was a full-time mom, but I couldn't help myself and gave myself fully to serving UPPERROOM.

The Question that Changed Everything

In 2012, I was leading worship one Sunday evening at UPPERROOM. We were starting the set with a song that was super popular in the Christian world at the time. I had seen it done at a conference and couldn't wait to try it out! I had this vision in my head that the

Spirit was gonna move like crazy, and we would all be on our faces by the end of the first song. So, we got into it, the musicians started playing, and we began singing the lyrics, "We wait for you."

Well, instead of it being epic, it felt like an epic failure. It was just plain rough! Even during the part where the drums went crazy and everyone should have been dancing, people were just standing around with blank stares on their faces. I couldn't wait for the song to end. We sang through the rest of the songs in the set, but I don't remember much else about it. The rest of the songs were probably fine, but I was just left confused. What happened? Why did I feel like we just trudged through mud?

Have you ever felt that way in worship? I led a lot of sets during that time, but I distinctly remember this one. I had a lot of questions, and those questions actually began a beautiful invitation.

In the early days, a guy named Traes Howard volunteered at the 6 am prayer set when they met in a corner of that room above the vet clinic. It overlooked the downtown area of Dallas, and every day, you could find him there, faithfully worshipping and praying over the city—often by himself. He was passionate about the Lord and started volunteering over prayer and worship with Michael and me. Eventually, Traes, Lorisa and I decided to meet weekly after the worship sets and talk about what happened at each service or prayer set. We'd ask questions like "Did you notice how the room shifted when we sang that song?", or "Did you feel what happened when that person said that?" We wanted to know why and talk about what could have been happening during those moments.

Traes knew about our releasing angels encounter, so we wanted to dive in further with that information and learn more about what it looks like to truly worship God. Why was the Lord's presence so strong and tangibly moving during certain songs, and why was it so dry at other times?

Just a quick note here: We weren't necessarily looking for people's reactions, although people *do* respond to the presence of God. There was just a clear distinction of what happened in different songs that marked our community. This caused us to really inquire with God because we wanted to understand what He was attracted to!

Through these debriefs, we realized that "vertical" worship felt more powerful. But using the term "vertical" to describe the type of worship it seemed God was attracted to just felt limited.

Around this same time, UPPERROOM started growing. We had no sign on the building, no cameras, and a website that had no information apart from our address, but God's hand was so evident that people started driving in from different cities just to experience Him. We started praying as a staff for blueprints for our church as we were still figuring out what God wanted to build in our midst. What was the Lord asking of our little church/prayer house?

I still don't think I was on staff at this time, but I was booking all the worship and prayer sets, and I was 100% invested! I had crazy faith that the Lord was gonna give us blueprints. I'll never forget the moment that I was pacing in the prayer room, and I felt the Lord ask me, "What would it look like if you threw a banquet in honor of Me every time you meet?" It was such a simple yet profound question. So, I started thinking about what a banquet in honor of someone looked like.

I'd close my eyes and try to imagine the King sitting on stage at a banquet table where people were getting up and telling testimonies of what He had done. I started asking myself, "What songs would I sing if I was gonna throw a banquet in honor of Jesus? What stories would I tell?" Which also begged the question, "What would I *not* say or do?"

Armed with this revelation, we began laying out all the sheet music (yes, we used paper in the olden days) and reading the words to the songs out loud. We wanted to see if it was something we would read out loud at a banquet in honor of Jesus. Honestly, we were shocked at how hard it was to find songs that just honored the Lord.

A lot of the "worship" songs at that time talked more about what we were *going to do* for God or *what we wanted* from Him. The songs also seemed to talk more about our needs than anything, like the focus was on us and our personal lack instead of the Lord. As the desire grew to simply honor Him and talk about things that Jesus had done for us, the song choices suddenly felt limited.

We started to take notice that the songs or parts of songs where the presence of God would manifest in our worship sets were all songs that honored, thanked, and praised the Lord, and the lightbulb turned on. This one question changed *everything* for me! After the banquet revelation, I don't think I ever had the dream about missing Jesus again.

This shift in perspective helped us start placing Jesus at the center of our services, and everything became about Him, His nature, and what He had done for us. That one question—"What would it look like to throw a banquet in honor of Jesus?"—invited us all into a journey of discovering what it looks like to "minister to the Lord." Up until that point, I had only heard of people describing worship as "vertical" (talking to God) or "horizontal" (talking to the congregation). I had never heard of ministering to the Lord in worship, although it is definitely mentioned throughout the Word. (Deuteronomy 10:8, 1 Samuel 2:18, Acts 13: 2)

Needless to say, we were ready to just sing praise songs. So, we went on a hunt for them. At that time, like I said earlier, we had a hard time finding modern songs that simply praised God. The majority of the songs we found were songs sung during previous moves of God or revival days, which was another lightbulb moment for me. Something was happening in those revival times where people wrote and sang honest heartfelt praise to Him for what He was doing and what He had already done. I thought to myself, *If we can't find current songs that praise Him, then we had better start writing them!*

This was also when we started getting the revelation of the power of expressing thanksgiving to the Lord. So, of course, I searched high and low for songs that said "thank you." Sadly, I couldn't really find any of those either! That's when my passion for writing "thank you" songs began. It came from an honest and genuine desire to say "thank you" to Him corporately as we discovered the power of it together.

A Plane without Wings

I had a friend once tell me, "Man, starting a service without thanksgiving and praise feels like trying to fly a plane without wings. We can go really fast down that runway, but it doesn't ever feel like we ever lift off the ground." I thought that was a profound statement. When we sing about ourselves, what we want, need, and even what we would like to do for God, it keeps us focused on the ground. When we focus on Him, what He can do and has done, we take off into the heavenlies and see everything from a different perspective.

The Bible says "we are seated in Christ in heavenly places," but when we are focused on our circumstances, it keeps us and our needs/lack at the center of the conversation. Often, this inadvertently magnifies the *problem* instead of God. I've actually seen people pray themselves into doubt because they are staring at the problem, saying, "God, this problem is so big! I need you to come and fix it!" Sure, that is a true statement. We do need Him, and sometimes the problem *is* big.

But if we stay focused on the problem, the problem is what becomes magnified.

But you know what? I've never seen anyone praise themselves into doubt. If you are saying, "You met me in the past! You did it for David! You healed that person, and You said you are Healer, so I'm standing with Jehovah Rapha, who is who He says He is!"

Can you feel that shift? When we change our language and focus on God, faith starts to rise. When we praise, we magnify God. Our perspective of Him right-sizes and the problems we have get smaller in comparison to the God we serve. David says, "Come, let's magnify the Lord together" because he realized when we magnify something, it gets bigger in our eyes!

I Get It Now!

Now, I want to make it clear that just because our core leadership team started receiving a deep revelation of the power of thanks and praise, it didn't mean our other worship leaders, prayer leaders, volunteers, or the congregation fully understood. The lightbulb had gone on for us, but teaching, explaining, and finding language didn't happen overnight. I personally had a deep conviction because I experienced the power of praise for myself. I had also gone through a three-year season where praise wasn't the main focus, and my heart grew tired and dry. Now, I'm incredibly thankful for that season because it allowed me to see the difference between the two environments. Without that time and the recurring dreams, I may have never learned the power of praise!

Unfortunately, teaching others what we had experientially learned was not easy. We would sometimes say, "It's more caught than taught," and there is some truth to that. Everyone could feel the difference when the atmosphere of the room would change in our exuberant praise sessions but people didn't always know *why*. It wasn't the amount of times we repeated something, specific drum builds, or free-flowing music. It was a lot more relational: looking for what God was doing in the room through praise.

We started choosing songs that reminded us of how good He is, and then He'd highlight a phrase or an aspect of His character or nature. We would stay on that highlighted piece and let the Lord lead us through it. Again, this didn't happen overnight. It came with a lot of messy services of honest searching and seeking! When you are pioneering something and treading into new territory, it's not always neat and polished. You have to be willing to try and fail!

During that time, we always had a facilitator open the service and transition us out of worship. We had given worship leaders the freedom to participate as well, even if they weren't leading that particular set. If they felt something the Lord was doing, they knew they could go to the facilitator to share, who would then filter and watch/communicate with the leader onstage if that moment should be sung or shared.

I remember a few different times when someone sang something that was declarative but more about what we were gonna do for God. It would be fine for a moment, and then it would fall flat. Of course, we felt a little derailed, but learning through those times was imperative for us to grow! After all, it was new territory for us.

We also developed a culture of debriefing that was super helpful. After every prayer or worship set, we talked through what we felt the Lord was doing. It was important to celebrate the beautiful times as well as talk about what was confusing or felt off. Not every conversation was easy, but it helped us process and learn to discern as a team and look for the Lord in our sets.

Let me be clear: it took quite a bit of time and patience for the bulk of this to translate across the board.

We taught about thanksgiving and praise a lot in our services and the residency program (our ministry school before it was a school). We joked that we were pounding the same note on the piano over and over until it stuck! Although we felt like we were being clear, we probably weren't, as we were still learning to communicate the concepts effectively. Regardless of how much we talked about thanksgiving and praise, everyone had to have their own "aha" moment.

I remember going through our leaders' song lists for Sundays and saying, "Hey guys, there are three songs where we are asking God for something and only one song that actually praises God. Could we trade out one of those 'asking songs' for a 'praise song'?"

Years later, a few of them told me that they had sometimes felt frustrated, like we were limiting their creativity and stifling their expression. They didn't understand why we were asking this of them, but they did it anyway because they trusted us. But at some point, there was always an "Oh, I get it now!"

For whatever reason, it would "click," and I would never have to check their song list again. They became utterly convinced of the power of praise and thanksgiving to the point where I would hear them teaching it to other people. The first time I overheard one of them telling someone else, I almost cried. We had finally found language, and now they were teaching it to others!

To this day, not every set is full of glory clouds. There is no formula. This is still a relationship with God's Spirit, and there is so much more we can learn. But what we *did* discover was that the worship sets where we focused on Jesus the most were the sets that impacted us the most.

6

THE PROCESSION TO GOD'S PRESENCE

Michael

A Psalm for giving thanks: Make a joyful noise to the LORD, all the earth! Serve the LORD with gladness! Come into his presence with singing! Know that the LORD, he is God! It is he who made us, and we are his; we are his people, and the sheep of his pasture. Enter his gates with thanksgiving, and his courts with praise! Give thanks to him; bless his name! For the LORD is good; his steadfast love endures forever, and his faithfulness to all generations. (Psalm 100)

In Dallas, we had a small 3-bedroom home, and by the time we had our third child, our home started to feel claustrophobic. Fluorescent toys and bouncy things littered the floor, and it felt like the walls were closing in on me. Internal frustrations were mounting as our family grew, and I thought I surely might die one night tripping over one of those fluorescent monstrosities. Naturally, I began to voice complaints about how small and constraining everything felt.

Ironically, around this same time, I began getting revelation on the power of thanksgiving. So, I decided to start my day by focusing on three things that I was thankful for. Every morning, as soon as I woke up, I intentionally connected my heart to what I was saying so that I could literally feel it. I didn't want to just provide lip service and throw up some religious robotic "thank you" to the ceiling; I wanted to connect my heart to God.

One morning, after about 10 days or so of morning gratitude, I was sitting in the living room. Suddenly, I was overtaken by a moment of awe and wonder. I caught myself saying things like, "Wow, I love this house! Look at this shade of blue on the walls. It's beautiful!" The home even *felt* bigger!

Wait, what did I just say? What changed? I thought. It

was the same small house with the same ugly fluores-

cent toys and light blue-colored walls. Yet something
had changed in me!

Don't Darken Your Heart

Have you ever considered the question, "What is the
actual giving of thanks?" Here's my working definition
before we get into the nitty-gritty: It is, first and foremost, showing honor in response to an act of lovingk-
indness. It is an agreement with Heaven that life itself
is a gift from God. Thanksgiving is an act of pure humility that acknowledges what someone else has done,
and it absolutely destroys entitlement. The Word says
that God resists the proud but gives grace to the hum-
ble, so that must mean that thanksgiving is a way to
receive grace! In fact, the Greek word for thanksgiving,
*eucharist*o, contains the Greek word for grace, *charis*,
right in the middle of it!

Unless we realize what we've been given and that
Jesus is the reason for all of it, we won't be able to prop-
erly give thanks, nor experience the abundant life that
He desires for us! We need to receive His grace to empower us to be able to live like Christ. We can't do it on
our own!

Furthermore, it is not that God *needs* our thanksgiving. But our thanksgiving allows us to agree with the truth, and the truth sets us free. God doesn't give good gifts with an agenda or manipulate us into feeling like we owe Him something. His gifts are to liberate us into love, empower us, and help us to become more than conquerors.

Ultimately, thanksgiving gives God access to our hearts. However, the flip side of that is that our hearts can become hard if we don't. The first chapter of Romans has a challenging but enlightening word for us in regard to the danger of NOT giving thanks. Let's take a look at verses 19-24:

> *For what can be known about God is plain to them, because God has shown it to them. For his invisible attributes, namely, his eternal power and divine nature, have been clearly perceived, ever since the creation of the world, in the things that have been made. So they are without excuse. For although they knew God, they did not honor him as God or give thanks to him, but they became futile in their thinking, and their foolish hearts were darkened. Claiming to be wise, they became fools, and exchanged the glory of the immortal God for images resembling mortal man and birds and animals and creeping*

things. Therefore God gave them up in the lusts of their hearts to impurity, to the dishonoring of their bodies among themselves, because they exchanged the truth about God for a lie and worshiped and served the creature rather than the Creator, who is blessed forever! Amen.

There are a few things I want to highlight here. First, this passage states that the attributes of God are plainly seen in nature. We have no excuse for not acknowledging the Creator. And we see here that because people didn't honor God (praise) or give thanks, *their hearts were darkened,* and they became fools. We took this to heart when praying for the area surrounding UPPERROOM at the time. The neighborhood the church was planted in was filled with people much like the ones in the passage above who worshipped the animal nature and were given over to their own lustful passions. So, our church decided to focus on the simplicity of honoring God and giving Him thanks daily, since that's what was missing in the people the Apostle Paul was describing in Romans.

If being ungrateful darkens our hearts, then gratitude must *illuminate* our hearts! In Ephesians 1, the Apostle Paul states that he doesn't cease to give thanks for the believers and that his desire was for the "eyes of their hearts to be enlightened." When the eyes of our hearts are enlightened, it affects how we see. Looking back at how I saw my home when I felt it was small and claustrophobic compared to when I started seeing my home as beautiful, it's obvious to me now that the only thing that changed was *how* I saw my home. In the former, my heart was darkened, and I was seeing with my physical eyes. In the latter, my heart was enlightened through thanksgiving, and I could see with the eyes of my heart.

Gratitude not only has an effect on your mind and heart, but it also has an effect on your physical body. Researchers at the Universities of Utah and Kentucky observed that stressed-out law students who characterized themselves as optimistic actually had more disease-fighting cells in their bodies.[2] Thanksgiving puts our cells on the offensive to destroy darkness within. That's powerful!

Gratitude Ushers in the Kingdom

When King David began to rule, one of the first decisions he made was to go after the ark of God's presence in 1 Chronicles 13:3, and to make Him the priority in Israel once again. In doing so, he created a tent of worship which we call David's tabernacle, where he put an exorbitant amount of focus, time, and resources towards the act of giving thanks. 1 Chronicles 16:7 says, "Then that day, David first appointed that thanksgiving be sung to the Lord by Asaph and his brothers." Next, in verses 41 and 42, we see that he chose certain people whose entire job was to "give thanks"! Then, the very first song sung in the tent was a song of thanksgiving. That's a lot of focus on gratitude!

All of this attention to gratitude begs the question, "Why"?

I think there are many reasons, but first and foremost, it's the gateway to God! It's how we enter in—we enter His gates with thanksgiving, which opens our hearts to God (Psalm 100:4). I know many will say, "But Michael, we have God with us all the time." To which I would say, "Yes, but how aware are you of God at all times?" It's important to note that there is also a difference between the *indwelling* presence of God and the *manifest* presence of God.

I'll never forget a moment that happened while I was teaching a residency class at UPPERROOM. It was the last day of school for the year, and the mother of one of the students was in the room. While I was teaching, I was prompted to pray for her and bless her with the money I had in my wallet. I didn't know it at the time, but she had been in a tough financial season. Once I opened my wallet, it prompted others to start giving to her as well. All of the spontaneous giving caused her to begin to weep with gratitude as the tangible presence of God filled the room. Many of us began to weep as well.

However, one young lady came to me and said, "Please pray for me. My heart is closing off. Something in me is wanting to run out of this classroom." As I started to pray for her, she let out a blood-curdling groan at the top of her lungs, her voice almost like a man's. The entire room turned their attention to me, praying for her, and a few of them came around to intercede. We tried to ask her questions, but all she could do was scream and groan. One of my friends, Lee Adams, said to her, "Say Jesus is Lord."

She tried with all her might, but all she could get out was, "Ju, Ju, Ju, Ju, Ju" and went back to screaming and jostling her body back and forth. It was a full-on demonic manifestation that was getting out of hand, as she had no control over her body or emotions. She couldn't even control her own speech! I Corinthians 12:3 says, "Therefore I want you to understand that no one speaking in the Spirit of God ever says "Jesus is accursed!" and **no one can say "Jesus is Lord" except in** the Holy Spirit." That verse had never been so real to me.

I began to pray and ask the Lord what to do, and I was able to recall a story she had told me about her mother. She had shared that her mother had a spirit of insanity, and she had felt that it was trying to come upon her. So, I decided to pray in that direction. I said, "Spirit of insanity, I command you in the name of Jesus to leave! Holy Spirit, come fill her!" All of a sudden, her tongue was loosed, and she said in her rightful voice, "Jesus is Lord!" She was totally set free in a moment.

It was unreal, but it taught me about the power of giving, open hearts, and what it all ushers in. The simple act of giving to that mother led to unbridled thanksgiving, and the Kingdom of God came into the room. When Jesus walked the earth and stepped foot in certain places, not only were people healed and set free, but it also caused demons to manifest! Those demons manifested because they couldn't stand the presence of God, and they knew it was time for them to go.

Practice Thanksgiving, Practice Peace

Thanksgiving ushers in the Kingdom of God, but it is also the doorway to His peace! Philippians 4:4-9 says,

"Rejoice in the Lord always; again I will say, rejoice. Let your reasonableness be known to everyone. The Lord is at hand; do not be anxious about anything, but in everything by prayer and supplication **with thanksgiving** let your requests be made known to God. And the peace of God, which surpasses all understanding, will guard your hearts and your minds in Christ Jesus."

We all need peace as much as the other person, but as the leader of a nation, it was *vital* for David's decision-making with so much on the line. Think of all the pressure that comes with ruling a nation, especially when your enemies are on the hunt against you! He needed to stay above the fray and remain in a place of clarity. David understood the power and had a massive value for gratitude.

Thankfully, gratitude and anxiety can't exist together. In fact, it's impossible to be grateful and anxious at the same time. Could it be that our anxieties and concerns overtake us because we lose the practice and mindset of gratitude? Science shows that when we express gratitude—or even *receive* gratitude—our brain releases dopamine and serotonin. These are neurotransmitters responsible for our emotions, and they make us feel good! They enhance our mood immediately. With constant gratitude, we can help the positive neural pathways to strengthen themselves and ultimately create a permanent grateful and positive nature within us.[3]

Early on in our marriage, Meredith and I created a gratitude habit together. Whenever we found ourselves in a discouraged mental hole, we took out a pen and paper and listed about 20-25 things that we were thankful for. Then we would shout them out Korean-style: at the same time, as loud as you can, for as long as you can. If you've never heard a group of Koreans pray before, you are missing out! They don't play when they pray. Everyone prays at the top of their lungs at the same time. It is thunderous!

Without fail, when we begin to shout out what we are thankful for, the atmosphere begins to shift around us. A smile emerges on our faces because it feels foolish, and then, all of a sudden, our hearts and minds begin to loosen up as we start to see and think differently. Sometimes it takes that aggressive style to bring the breakthrough because anxiety tries to intimidate us into a shrunken, timid, muted, docile version of ourselves.

Thanksgiving was also a key part of Jesus's lifestyle and a precursor to His miracles. The most obvious example is the miracle of the loaves and fishes. It was at the time of Passover, and there were thousands gathered to Jesus as he was teaching them. Jesus asked the disciples how they were going to feed such a multitude, but they responded that they didn't have enough money or food. Andrew sheepishly offered that there was a young boy who had five barley loaves and two fish. The Bible says that there were 5,000 men in attendance, but that didn't include the women and children.

John 6:11 says, "Jesus then took the loaves, and **when he had given thanks**, he distributed them to those who were seated. So also the fish, as much as they wanted." The next day, more people began to arrive, and John 6:23 tells us more of the story: "Other boats from Tiberias came near the place where they had eaten the bread **after the Lord had given thanks**."

Notice that last phrase: the place where they had eaten bread after the Lord gave thanks. It doesn't say, "the place where the miracle of multiplication took place." To me, that would be a more fitting statement. But from John's perspective, and possibly even God's perspective, this was the place where thanks was given. In an impossible situation, thanksgiving made a way for a miracle to occur!

I'm sure it looked pretty foolish to the disciples after looking at a crowd of over 5,000. All Jesus had was two little ol' fish and five measly pieces of bread. But he chose to give God thanks for the little that he had. Man, that takes some foolish faith! 1 Thessalonians 5:16-18 says, "Rejoice always, pray without ceasing, **give thanks in all circumstances**; for this is the will of God in Christ Jesus for you." Giving thanks in all circumstances is God's will for your life, and the results speak for themselves. After all, if Jesus did it, then so should we!

Earlier in the book, I mentioned 2 Chronicles 20 and the battle of Jehoshaphat. It's a pretty famous story with regard to sending the worshippers into battle first before the army and God using it to confuse their enemies into killing each other. But have you ever looked at what they are singing as they go into battle with no weapons other than their instruments? You'd imagine they were singing some aggressive song like "Enter Sandman," but no.

Check out the lyrics: "Give thanks to the Lord. His love endures forever." They're singing a thank you song right into the battlefield. Imagine being in that band, and as you are staring across the battlefield at an enraged horde, your leader says, "Cue the 'Thank You' song!" In *my* head, I'm thinking that I'm marching to my death while singing thank you! I'd be like, "Um sir, how about something with a little more of a war feel to it, possibly? Could we at least sing something to give us some courage?" I could imagine him saying, "Yes, that is why you need to sing a song of thanks because anxiety and gratitude can't exist together! Plus, it takes faith to sing that in the face of your enemies. Watch what God does!" The power of thanksgiving in your greatest battles can't be overstated!

Then there's Jonah. Have you ever really read Jonah, or do you consider it to be some crazy children's story? I mean, after all, he's running from God's will and ends up in the belly of a whale in the depths of the ocean. It seems pretty silly to the natural mind. However, there is an insightful metaphor here if you look a little deeper. God had called Jonah to preach a message of repentance to Nineveh for their wicked ways, and Jonah didn't want to do it! He ran away from the presence of the Lord and gets on a ship to attempt to sail far away from Ninevah. A storm ensues, and Jonah confesses to the sailors that the life-threatening situation they are in is his fault for running from the presence of God. They cast him overboard, and as if things couldn't get any worse, a great fish "appointed by God" swallowed him up!

What the story is trying to illustrate to you (among other things) is that if you run from God's will, you will end up in a pretty deep and dark place!

But do you know what caused Jonah to get out of that situation? After three days in the belly of that great fish, he somehow comes to his senses and says in Jonah 2:9, "But I with the voice of thanksgiving will sacrifice to you." I tell you what, it's definitely not easy to give thanks in the darkest moments of your life, but look at what could happen when you do.

Check out what Jonah 2:10 says: "And the LORD spoke to the fish, and it vomited Jonah out upon the dry land." *Immediately* after he offers up thanks, that fish spits him out onto dry land, right back on track toward Nineveh, the place of his destiny. Can thanksgiving launch you out of darkness? It sure did for me!

Don't Be a Groundhog

There is an exhortation in the Bible mentioned in Psalms 95:8 and Hebrews 3:15 that says, "Don't harden your hearts as they did in the wilderness." The authors of these books understood that one of the things that kept the Israelites stuck in the wilderness was that their hearts were hard. This happened because they began to complain to one another about their situation, and it was infectious. Instead of giving a *thank offering* in the wilderness, they gave a *stank offering* of complaints! In times of transition or difficult seasons, complaining will be tempting. However, in the face of these situations, it makes it all the more powerful to give thanks and praise because it's in opposition to the flesh!

Have you ever seen the movie *Groundhog Day*? It's about a weatherman who keeps having the same day over and over again. In the film, he has to report on the tradition of the groundhog. If the groundhog sees its shadow, winter goes on for six more weeks. In the movie, the groundhog is a metaphor for the weatherman played by Bill Murray's character, Phil Connor. He's constantly staring at the shadows and sees the negative in everything. And because of that, he keeps having the same day over and over and over and over again, stuck in winter, so to speak. Or, in the case of the Israelites, the wilderness.

That being said, every single morning, God's grace was calling out to him on a radio alarm clock with a song that sang, "Put your little hand in mine. There ain't no hill or mountain we can't climb. Babe, bum bum, bum bum, I got you, babe, bum bum." God was calling out to him, but he couldn't quite see or hear it because he was complaining about everybody and everything. He was staring at the shadows.

Andy McDowell stars as the character played opposite Phil, and her name in the movie is Rita. The name Rita means "bringer of light." She begins to live out her name by teaching him about 14th-century French poetry, love, and kindness, which he sees as sentimental dribble. Phil's name comes from the Greek word *phileo*, which means *love*; however, he doesn't know that that's his true identity. So, the bringer of light comes to bring him his true identity. She begins to teach him about love, and once he has this revelation, he's like, "Wait a minute!"

One night, while reading poetry to Rita, he has a revelation and says, "What if God made the tree?" All of a sudden something clicks, and he begins to see life as a gift. So, he begins to serve humanity and beautify the earth. All of a sudden, he wakes up on a new day and no longer hears that same song because he actually believes it!

I believe the same is true for us. We can be stuck in these same seasons because we're still playing the old stories in our head. We're still focused on the shadows or the darkness of our stuck situations, but if we'll practice gratitude and praise and start our days that way, entering his gates as we arise, He'll break us into a new day so we don't get stuck in the wilderness. Then we can finally enter into the promised land and begin to do what we were created to do... slay giants!

This practice will change your life if you let it. So, before moving on to the next chapter, I have a challenge for you. Let's start today and give a little thanks! Make a list of 20 things you are thankful for, then shout them out Korean-style. Bonus points if you're with other people. I want you to notice how your heart and mind shift while you're doing it. It's the gateway to God's presence, after all!

Lastly, my wife has written a few songs of gratitude that are great to sing after you've reminded yourself what you are thankful for! Search for *Thank You Song*, or *You and You Alone*. You will be thankful that you did!

7

PRAISE IS PERSONAL

Meredith

ONE OF THE most important things we learned about praise in those seasons is that praise is "personal." Now, I don't mean "personal" as in "I'm not gonna share it with you" or "I'll keep it to myself" kind of personal. I mean that the more you know someone personally, the more personal the praise can be. If I try to praise a stranger I don't know on the street, I'm limited to what they are wearing or their nice smile because I don't know them personally. My mother, on the other hand, is someone I could never run out of praise for—not only because she has done so much for me over the years, but because I know her so well!

Before we get deeper into how we make praise personal, it's helpful to define what praise is and what it is not. After all, for a long time, the church has defined "praise and worship" as any song we sing at church. And, oftentimes, praise was further defined as the "fast" songs.

When you break it down in the Bible, praise is pretty specific. There are seven Hebrew words for praise, and they all speak to different forms of praise.

1. **Towdah:** To lift your hands in thanksgiving (Exodus 27:6-7, Romans 12:1)

2. **Yadah:** To raise or throw up your hands (Exodus 17:11, 1 Timothy 2:8)

3. **Barak:** To kneel or bless in reverence (Exodus 34:8, Psalm 5:7)

4. **Halal:** To rejoice or to boast clamorously—this is anything but quiet! (Psalm 149:3, 2 Samuel 6:14)

5. **Zamar:** To praise with instruments (Psalm 150: 3-5, Ephesians 5:19

6. **Tehillah:** To praise with spontaneous or unprepared songs (Psalm 22:25; Isaiah 61: 1-3)

7. **Shabach:** To shout for joy (Psalm 47:1, Isaiah 12:6).

As you can see, there are so many beautiful ways to express our praise. All these words give us so much permission to jump, dance, shout, and spontaneously sing our heart song to the Lord.

I want to dig in a little more and say that these are ways to *express* praise, but they are not true definitions. So, what exactly is praise? Here is a quick definition from Oxford Languages: "The expression of approval or admiration for someone or something; to express warm approval or admiration of." So, if praise is about admiration of who God is and what He has done, then that is pretty specific!

As I started to mention earlier, the church often categorizes the "praise song" as the fast song you open with and get everyone to clap to so you can make sure they're awake to start church. But praise is actually way more about *what* we are saying than a specific tempo! (Yes, I know what a "praise break" is in gospel terms, but that's not what I'm talking about here!)

Though the differences are not in tempo, there *are* actually a lot of different types of songs we sing in church. I'll quickly mention a few:

- **Prayer songs** where we are collectively asking God to do something or singing our prayers.

Think of songs that sing through something like the Lord's Prayer.

- **Declaration songs** that focus more on what we are going to do for the Lord, singing things like, "I'm gonna run to You." There are also declaration songs declaring what the *Lord* is going to do.
- **Prophetic songs** that are singing what the Lord is saying to the church.

All of these types of songs and more have a place in services, but they are not necessarily praise. Let me give you an example of what we often do in our sets and label as praise so you know what I mean.

I'm Gonna Praise You

When I'm teaching in different places or leading a SongLab, there's a point when I usually make my husband come to the front of the room. It goes something like this:

"I'm going to praise my husband, Michael, right now. You ready?" I make sure we're facing each other and flash a big smile as I look at him lovingly.

"Okay, Michael. I'm waiting for you. I'm gonna run to you. Break my chains. I need you, and I'm really lost without you. I'm gonna praise you! I *will* praise you!"

People typically start laughing, starting to understand the illustration before I get to the punchline.

"Alright, how do you feel about Michael after that? Do you know any more about him? Is your heart open to him? Probably not. You might know more about what *I* need and want, but you don't know much about Michael.

"Now, are these things wrong to say? Absolutely not. Those statements have their place, but my point is that those statements are not praise."

Are you, the reader, getting it already? I'm sure you are. So, let's try that again.

"Michael, I'll never forget the day we stood on the street corner in Turkey when I was breaking down in the biggest ugly mess, even blaming you for my feelings, and you didn't walk away. You stood there in my tantrum and represented Jesus like I had never experienced before. You continually show me characteristics of God's unconditional love. You walk with integrity, and when you say something, I can take it to the bank. You are fun and intentional, and the best father our kids could ever have. They want to be with you and around you because you love them so well. You are my favorite person, and I love the adventures you take us on. I can trust you because you follow Jesus with your all!"

After this demonstration, Michael usually has tears welling up in his eyes, and everyone in the room applauds. Why? Because true praise is moving! Most of the people in the room don't know Michael from Adam, but there is something about authentic and personal praise that opens the hearts of *everyone*.

This is precisely why your testimonies are so powerful because they are *your* stories of *your* encounters of how Jesus met you! It's *your* praise, and it's personal. To take this further, let me say this: I can't sing your praises for you. Yes, if you write a song and I sing it, I'm technically singing your praise. But it means something different to me when I'm singing it. I'm putting my heart and story into your song, but your praise to Him moves His heart because it's your story with God. You have the history behind it!

Some of the most memorable moments in our early days at UPPERROOM services were when we would worship for a while and then throw out all our plans and open it up for people to share testimonies. I have always admired Michael Miller for being willing to throw out the plans to flow in what He felt the Lord was doing in the room. We would worship between testimonies, and I'm telling you, the songs and praise would get more and more exuberant because it's hard not to dance, clap, and shout when you hear what people have been saved, healed, and delivered from! The songs took on new meaning after each testimony was shared. I truly believe Heaven is attracted to the praise of Jesus!

On one of our Sunday evenings like I just described, a literal cloud came into the room! It was like a fog of pure peace and joy. I think that service went on for hours, and it felt like minutes. As a kid, I remember thinking that having to sit on a cloud and worship for eternity would be super boring. But, after sitting in services like what we experienced, I don't think anything could be better than worshipping Jesus for eternity. It felt like heaven joined us in that room! We were learning the power of praise, and I was ruined for anything else. I couldn't get enough.

How Do You Know Him?

Here is where I want to get practical! I want you to do something with me for a moment: Let's make it personal right now. I want you to take a few minutes and think about one of your favorite characteristics about God. I know there are so many things, but what is something that just moves you? Is it His faithfulness when others have not been faithful? Is it His patience to pursue you when you kept running? Is it His peace in the middle of chaos, or the way He shows up as your Father when you need one?

Now, with that characteristic in mind, if I asked you why you chose that one, you would most likely have a story to tell. You might tell of a time when He met you—an encounter you had with Him as a Father, and the story behind it all. The characteristic you described earlier might be as simple as "His faithfulness," but behind that common phrase, there is a personal moment! So, when you sing or say the phrase, "I love Your faithfulness," it carries weight because it's personal. It comes from a moment with Him. It's not a concept anymore—you *know* Him as faithful!

You can see this played out when you have two different singers singing the same song. One of them might have a really great voice and sings the song technically well, but then the other singer, who may not be as technically good of a singer, sings with every fiber of their being, and the whole room is floored. Most of the time, we can actually *feel* the difference. The authentic, whole-hearted singer carries an anointing because they aren't singing from a concept; they are singing from conviction.

I believe anointing often comes when a truth has been lived out. When we have experienced a specific aspect of the Lord, it's no longer just head knowledge; it's a heart knowing.

God isn't looking for robots going through the motions, repeating the right thing to say. If our "praise" is just empty words that don't mean anything to us, do we think it's gonna mean something to Him? Hosea 6:6 says, "For I desire steadfast love and not sacrifice, the knowledge of God rather than burnt offering." He wants our hearts, and He wants us to know Him, not just go through the motions of things we think we should say out of religious duty.

Make Him the Host

When we engage personally in praise to Him that moves *our* hearts, we sing authentically. That's when we have found that Jesus shows up!

I remember one of my worship leaders coming to me when our services were really exploding, and people were driving in from all over the place. We started feeling pressure as the spotlight was beginning to shine on our community. When the lights came on to the UPPERROOM, we found that exposure exposes.

It exposes our insecurities and things we didn't know were there, but it also exposes good things.

During this exposing season, one of the worship leaders said something along the lines of, "I'm feeling a lot of pressure. How do I pick songs?" The answer was simple. I told her, "Pick the songs that make your heart open to the Lord." Almost immediately, she let out a big sigh of relief as the pressure lifted.

Another question that emerged was one I'm sure lots of worship leaders wrestle with: "How do you pick a song for the congregation when you know some people are in the worst season of their life while others are having the best season? How do you pick songs to meet both groups?" My answer came from the revelation we were receiving when making a note about what singing praise was opening up in our services.

"You don't pick songs for them; you pick songs for Him. Then when He comes into the room, He meets both groups where they are!"

When we choose to invite Him as the guest of honor to the banquet we throw Him, incredible things happen. We sing songs to Him that describe what moves us about Him, and He takes over the service and becomes the host! When He is in the driver's seat, it is so much better than anything we could put together ourselves. He meets people in ways we could never meet them, and lives are changed forever!

Now, let's get into Michael's side of praise.

Michael

I like to geek out on the Hebrew versions of words. In Genesis 4:1, it says, "now Adam **knew** Eve, his wife, and she conceived and bore Cain." She bore a child out of this "knowing" of each other. This word *knew* is the Hebrew word *yada,* which speaks of intimacy in such a way that life comes forth, if you catch my drift. So, they knew God, and they knew one another—they were intimate with each other. This is yada. This knowing is an intimate oneness.

One of the Hebrew words for praise is *yadah*. Look familiar? It's essentially the word *knew*, as in *yada*, with the Hebrew letter *hèh* attached to it. *Hèh* is symbolic of the Spirit of God because when you say *hèh,* it sounds like breath, and breath and Spirit are synonymous. For instance, when Abram encountered God, he became Abraham because he had encountered the Spirit of God, which changed him. When his wife Sara encountered the Spirit of God, she became Sarah.

Well, when *we* encounter God, we become intimate with Him. We know Him. This is a yada knowing. From that knowing, when we pour our praise back to Him, that *yada* becomes *yadah*. *Yadah* is one of the seven Hebrew words for *praise*, and consists of three Hebrew letters. Hebrew letters are also pictures as well as numbers. So, there are multidimensional layers to what a Hebrew letter is.

When you look at the word *yadah* from a visual imagery standpoint, something unique emerges! It consists of three consonant letters since there are no vowels in the Hebrew alphabet. The first letter is *yod*, and the imagery of *yod* is a picture of hands being extended. *Dalet* is the middle letter, and the imagery of *dalet* is the picture of a door opening. Lastly, the third letter is *heh*. It is the picture of the Spirit or breath of God entering in. When you put these three letter images together, you have hands being extended, a door opening, and the Spirit of God coming in.

Pretty interesting, huh? As you turn your encounters of personal intimacy back to God in praise, your heart opens to allow the Spirit of God to come in!

Praise is a Sacrifice

One of the aspects of praise that I noticed over time was the sacrificial dimension to it. The time my wife and I spent in Israel was such a formational season for

our faith *and* our marriage. One of the key phrases we learned there was that "conflict brings intimacy." Of course, conflict can—and often does—bring the opposite of that. But in the Kingdom of God and in our marriages, the goal is always intimacy! It's super helpful to have that mindset because conflict will arise in our closest relationships, especially marriage.

One night in our small 2-bedroom apartment back in Dallas, we found ourselves in a conflict. I honestly don't even recall what we were arguing over, but we were struggling to find common ground and get to the truth of the matter. I don't know about you, but I'm not a fan of conflict being that I'm a feeler. I'm not afraid of it, but I don't like it. Conflict isn't comfortable, and I hate the way it feels.

So, I came up with a brilliant idea. I asked her if she wanted to go get some ice cream! I wanted something sweet to soothe the bitterness of what I was feeling in the moment. That was *not* like me because I rarely eat sweets. She looked at me with this odd head tilt and said, "We should probably praise the Lord."

That statement infuriated me. I wanted to soothe my flesh, and she had this holy idea. My flesh was burning, but I understood that the spirit and the flesh are in opposition to one another. Soon enough, something rose within me, and I aggressively declared war against the flesh.

"That's the last thing I want to do," I said. "Let's do it!"

We both awkwardly began to give thanks and praise God at the top of our lungs. It wasn't too much longer when something suddenly broke and the atmosphere shifted as the presence of God was manifest in the room. It's not that we could see God with our physical eyes, but we could sense His presence. It was holy and liberating, and the frustration left as the Prince of Peace entered the room.

All of a sudden, revelation started coming to both of us. I grabbed my pen and journal and began to write what I was hearing from the Lord, and when I glanced over my shoulder to see why I wasn't hearing her praise any longer, I saw that she was journaling, too! Psalm 22 states that God dwells in the praises of His people, and we were experiencing that reality in our small apartment.

There was definitely a sacrificial dimension to what we did. It was a sacrifice of praise because it was literally the last thing that I wanted to do! My flesh wanted to be coddled, but my spirit wanted to override that desire by sacrificing the pleasures of the flesh. And that's when God showed up.

Think about the Old Testament. They would sacrifice by burning animal flesh on the altar. You know what happens when you offer up a sacrifice of praise when your fleshly nature wants to be coddled? Your flesh burns!

God always has a higher way of doing things, but often in our frustrations, we make the wrong decisions and shut the door to His help. So let's flip the script! Hebrews 13:15 says, "Through him, then let us continually offer up a sacrifice of praise to God, the fruit of our lips that acknowledge his name through him." How often should we offer up a sacrifice of praise to God? Continually.

So, how do we practically do that?

The 2020 Hindsight

The year was 2020. The coronavirus had broken out in China, and the news began 24/7 coverage of people around the world dying. I was walking through the airport in Dallas on a layover heading to Atlanta from San Antonio when I noticed a few people wearing masks in the airport. All of the TVs in the airport were pumping out fear-based coverage of the outbreak. Out of nowhere, I was blanketed by a coat of fear covering my body. I felt as if I were in the grip of the shadows of death. Tormenting thoughts began to assault my mind and heart.

Could this be the end?

Then it was as if my spirit man rose up and back slapped me with a fist full of faith. Bubbling up first from within my gut, then gushing forth from my mouth, I began to declare, "Lord, You said no pestilence shall come near my dwelling! Sickness is not my portion! You are my shield, You are my fortress, You are my very great reward!" I could almost hear a snap in the spirit realm as fear broke off me and dissipated. I felt like a live wire as every hair on my body shot out like Einstein's hair. For the next 15-20 minutes, I walked through the airport and felt an impenetrable force of God engulfing my body. I was no longer in the shadow of death, but I was under the shadow of His wings! God was inhabiting my praise, and it was so much more powerful than the weak presence of fear and darkness.

Later on that year, a global pandemic was officially declared as the entire world became hyper-focused on a virus, and much of the world shut down. Fear was the prevailing wind that dictated the world's responses. There was 24/7 coverage, making sure every case was shown like a stock ticker on all the news channels. Everyone was masked up within a short amount of time as they were made hyper-aware of something they couldn't actually see. It dominated our thinking and our conversations, and it was as if we were continually offering up a sacrifice of praise to the power of this virus.

Before that year began, I was seeking God for words for what the year ahead may hold for me and my family. The word that I felt God was speaking to me was, "My people need courage." Little did I know how much courage was going to be an asset in the days ahead because of how much fear was peddled through the media.

Thankfully, one of the things that the COVID season really taught me was how to praise on a whole other level. It was definitely more consistent because I noticed how I was continually being made aware of the virus. From the constant barrage in the media to everyone wearing masks, it was being magnified through fear.

I remember having this thought: *I'm not gonna allow the awareness of this little virus to take dominance in my mind over the reality of God.* So, the minute I would start to feel or sense fear, I would just begin to magnify and praise God in the midst of it. I was walking in the opposite spirit, offering up a sacrifice of praise! I began stewarding His presence to a degree I'd never known.

All that to say, I began to look at all of life's challenges as opportunities to offer up a sacrifice of praise, which thrust me fully into the awareness and presence of Almighty God!

Patrick and Praise

One year, Meredith and I had the privilege of going to Ireland and tracing the steps of St. Patrick all over the country. As the story goes, Patrick had this relationship with the Lord where he was said to have prayed over a hundred prayers a day. He had a beautiful, powerful prayer called the Lorica of Patrick. I encourage you to look it up sometime. As a child, he grew up as a slave in Ireland but escaped back to his homeland in what is modern-day Britain. While he was home, the Lord spoke to him about returning to the land where he had been a slave to share the Gospel with them. So, he courageously went back.

During his day, he saw almost an entire nation converted to Christianity. There are stories of these power encounters with druids, pagans, and people coming to Christ in masses. From his generation onward, there were monasteries established like Bangor Abbey, which had nonstop, 24/7 prayer and praise for nearly 200 years! These early Celtic Christians said that the key to their power in Ireland was what they would describe as *Laus Perennis*. Laus Perennis is a Gaelic phrase that means *continual praise*. Stumbling into these historical clues caused us to take a deeper look into the various dimensions of praise and what it looked like practically to walk it out.

This Is NOT What I Signed Up For

One of my favorite stories in the Bible is one that I briefly mentioned earlier in the book. It's the story of Paul and Silas in Acts 16. The guys were on a missionary journey together, and one day, they were heading to the place of prayer. This was a part of their daily routine. While en route, they were intercepted by a slave girl who had a spirit of divination, and the Bible says that she brought her owners much gain by her fortune telling. Basically, she was the source of income for some wealthy, influential people in Macedonia. She followed Paul and Silas for days, yelling out things about them, and it eventually wore Paul out.

Verse 18 says that Paul became greatly annoyed and cast the demon out of the girl.

Now, this sent her owners into a bit of a tizzy. Their meal ticket was sent home packing, which threw them into a rage against Paul and Silas. They proceeded to drag Paul and Silas into the center of town in front of the rulers and began to throw accusations against them. This riled up the crowd, who then decided to mob them, strip them naked, and beat them with rods. After the beating, they were put into the local first-century dank, smelly prison with their feet fashioned into stocks.

At this point, it was about midnight. Of course, that was the actual time, but it's also symbolic of one's darkest hour. Put yourself into this situation for a moment. What would a natural human response be in that situation? I don't know about you, but as I mentioned earlier in the book, I'd probably be whining to God, asking questions like, "Where are You, Lord? Is this what You give me for doing Your will? We've been preaching the Gospel, and this is our reward? Yeah God, this is not what I signed up for."

I mean, think about it. Their situation is intense. There is no way on earth that they didn't *want to* complain. But what did they do? It says that around midnight, at their darkest hour, they began to pray and sing hymns of praise to God. I mean, talk about a sacrifice! In their flesh, there is no way that they "felt" like praising God.

As a result of this crazy out-of-this-world sacrifice of praise, Acts 16:26 says, "and suddenly there was a great earthquake, so that the foundations of the prison were shaken. And immediately all the doors were opened, and everyone's bonds were unfastened."

Yes, this is a literal story, but it's also applicable to our own lives. When we feel that our world is closing in on us, like we're in our darkest hour, praise is the gateway to God's presence. And, of course, where the Spirit of the Lord is, there is freedom!

It is Finished

The story of Paul and Silas caused me to ponder some things about their story and the life of Jesus. How did they know how to praise God in such a horrible situation? In my mind, this wasn't something instinctual. They knew something other-worldly. They understood the sacrifice of praise.

So, I started looking at the life of Jesus. I wondered what Jesus's "midnight hour" was. Gethsemane was dark, but what was darker? It was definitely when He was on the cross. That was, by far, His darkest hour. Now think about the position He was in while nailed to the cross. His arms were outstretched.

Then, what was the last thing Jesus said right before he gave up His spirit? He said with a loud voice, "My God, my God. Why have you forsaken me?" This sounds like a justified complaint. However, before it existed in the gospels, it was written as the first verse of Psalm 22. The third verse is where the imagery of what He's actually doing begins to come into focus: "Yet you are holy. The God who **dwells in the praises of his people**." The last verse of Psalm 22, which is clarified in the Passion Translation, states, "It is finished."

Get this: Jesus, in His darkest hour, is going through Psalm 22! He's actually lifting up a sacrifice of praise! Remember earlier when I was talking about *yadah* and its imagery of hands being extended, a door opening, and the Spirit of God being released? When Jesus said, "It is finished" and gave up His spirit, it says that the veil inside the actual temple was torn, and the Spirit of God was released into the earth.

But He wasn't done yet! As the Spirit permeated the earth, one of the first manifestations was that graves began to erupt in response, and people started bursting forth out of the graves! This imagery is so similar to when Paul and Silas were in prison lifting up a sacrifice of praise. People were being liberated from their shackles and prison cells!

Another fascinating note about Paul and Silas from their "prison break" situation is that when their prison bars and shackles were opened, they didn't leave. I would have thrown up the peace sign and sprinted for the hills. These guys were different. They knew that there was a bigger purpose for why they were there. Because they stayed, the prison guard and his entire family got saved!

This leaves me with a question for you. What if the trials and tribulations you find yourself in are for you to release the light and glory of God so that those around you might get set free from the prisons and graves they are trapped in? That brings an entirely different perspective and purpose to our trials, right? What would happen if we become radical people of praise like Paul and Silas? That through the darkest things we go through, we choose to lift up this sacrifice of praise, the heavens of God are opened, and the Spirit of God is released into our situations to set captives free?

Now, I'm not saying that it is easy. No sacrifice is. Could you imagine trying to sing through or scream through a Psalm when your lungs are collapsing as you hang beaten and bloody on a cross? You are barely able to breathe, so you have to push up on the nail in your feet to catch a breath so that you can sing out praise to God. It's almost impossible and incomprehensible, but when you realize that your praise comes from Him, you will have the grace for it at any given moment.

The Cloud of His Presence

Now that we've talked about giving a sacrifice of praise, let's talk about being hosts of His presence through our sacrifices, becoming living tabernacles He dwells in.

In 2005, we were still in Jerusalem with YWAM. This particular week, we had a Scottish teacher named Yolanda who was teaching on getting free from the fear of man. After her short teaching, she sat down, crossed her arms, and said, "The Holy Spirit is going to take over from here." We all just sat around looking at each other, wondering what was going to happen next.

At that time, my wife had never played guitar in front of people before, as she was just learning the instrument. But that particular morning, she "randomly" felt led to bring her guitar to class with her. After a couple of minutes of us staring at the teacher and each other, Meredith walked to the back of the room, picked up her guitar, sat down on a chair in front of the class, and began to play and sing a song. She was afraid and didn't want to do it, but she knew it was her door to break the fear of man. As she began to play, she lifted up her song to God. Not only was it beautiful, but it was liberating for *all of us* in the room. Her freedom was helping us all to get free!

Next, there was a woman in our class named Brigita. She had a mild form of cerebral palsy that caused her hands to curl inward. It was as if her hands were shackled, and it kept her in a prison of shame. After Meredith played and sang, Brigita stood in front of the class and said that she'd never danced before the Lord in worship, and she wanted to do it that day in front of all of us. So, she turned on a small portable speaker, put on some worship music, and began to dance. But she didn't just dance—she danced those shackles of fear off with all her might! Through her dance, she was lifting up a sacrifice of praise in front of everybody.

I'll never forget what happened next. As we watched her incredibly touching display of dance despite the fear and cerebral palsy, we all broke down in tears. It was as if the glory of God was beaming through her, and we couldn't take in the full beauty of it.

This next part may be hard to believe, but all of a sudden, the room appeared cloudy. It was as if a smoke machine had been turned on, and haze filled the lenses of our eyes. The glory of God had broken through and filled our room just like when the temple of Solomon was dedicated to the Lord! We couldn't believe our eyes, yet we couldn't stop crying and fell on our faces. Brigita, however, just continued as her dance became even more liberating!

In 2 Chronicles 5:13-14, Solomon's temple was completed, and it details how they were bringing the ark of God into the temple. Look at what it says:

It was the duty of the trumpeters and singers to make themselves heard in unison in praise and thanksgiving to the LORD, and when the song was raised, with trumpets and cymbals and other musical instruments, in praise to the LORD, "For he is good, for his steadfast love endures forever," the house, the house of the LORD, was filled with a cloud, so that the priests could not stand to minister because of the cloud, for the glory of the LORD filled the house of God.

I don't know about you, but that is a pretty wild and strange verse. A cloud filled the temple in the midst of

no longer have a physical ark for the Lord to rest upon,
but now we have become the living arks of His presence. See Acts 11:15 & 1 Corinthians 3:16

Let's Get Practical

Alright. You've now learned through Meredith about
praise being personal, and you've learned from my
side about bringing a sacrifice of praise and what it
means that we are now His temple. Now, I want to take
a moment for another practical exercise. We're going
to take some time and write a letter to God.

If you are in a good season, just write out what He
means to you, and make it personal. Write out a de-
tailed memory of how He's encountered you or impacted your life. It could be the way you met or gave
your life to Him, a healing testimony, anything!

If you are in a difficult season, which I expect more
people to resonate with, then it's time to write a sacrifice of praise! I don't know what your situation might
be, but let's say you are having financial issues. You
could ask yourself, "What are the fear-based thoughts
I'm having right now?" They could be things like: "I
don't know how I'm ever going to make money," "My
business is failing, and I can't stop the decline," or "I've
got more expenses than my income can handle."

Whatever they may be, you need to find some Scriptures that declare the opposite! For example, "My Bible says that God owns the cattle on a thousand hills, so He's not strapped for cash." Also, look to times in the past where He's come through for you and write that out. Then, ask Him what part of His nature He wants to reveal to you in this season. It could be that He is Provider, it could be the promise of His peace, or something else altogether.

After you have written your letter, set an empty chair across from you. Then read that letter out to God as if He were in that chair. You should notice your heart opening to God. If you are in a difficult season, your perspective should be shifting from fear to faith!

As you become more aware of God than your situation, or stated another way, as He becomes bigger in your mind and heart than the problems you are going through, just take some time and talk to Him. He wants to know (yada) you more, so you can lift up more praise!

8

WHAT IS GOD SEARCHING FOR?

Meredith

BEFORE WE GET too far into this chapter, I want to address something. Parts of this chapter *are* written with worship leaders in mind. However, if that's not you, I don't want you to check out. Even if you don't currently lead worship or sing or play a lick of anything, the information here will inform your congregational worship experience. Remember, my husband doesn't sing (well) or play an instrument! Aside from that, you are called to be a worshipper. Period! There are truths here for everyone to glean.

So, now that we got that out of the way, let's get into it.

If you have been a believer for any amount of time, you have probably gone through some things. (Or some *thaaangs!*) In fact, suffering is actually promised in this life of following Jesus (James 1:3). During seasons of trial, praise can sometimes feel dishonest or inauthentic because we don't actually "feel" like praising God. It's understandable, right? When you're in the thick of it, praise is often the last thing your flesh feels like doing, as Michael has described in detail.

I've had this conversation with quite a few different leaders at different times, as it can feel hypocritical to be leading people when you aren't feeling it. If you're hurting or navigating difficult circumstances in your personal life, how do you show up to lead other people? This is what we have discovered: It is never hypocritical to agree with the truth! Our feelings change with circumstances—they can even turn around with a snack and a good nap—but truth is not based on feelings. It's based on the man Jesus, who *is* Truth. This Truth is unshakable, and it is infinitely greater than our circumstances and feelings.

I have found that when we align with who He is *in spite of* how we feel, our spirits start to align with the truth—Jesus—over the "facts" about our circumstances. I've even found that some of the most powerful times of worship have come from a place like this: "God, I don't feel like You are good or faithful right now, but I know Your Word says that You are. So, despite how I feel, I'm gonna sing these songs 'til my heart lines up with Your reality."

Remember what Michael shared about offering a sacrifice of praise? These are the times that sacrifice truly becomes real. The times when it isn't easy, when you haven't felt a breakthrough, and when it actually feels costly to show up and sing about the character and nature of God. To take that a step further, this is the only time that we get to offer God something in the midst of pain. Our *choice* to praise when darkness seems to be winning is our most powerful act of warfare! I also believe this is the kind of praise that releases angels to fight on our behalf. Having now walked with God for a long time, I know that when all hell seems to have been unleashed, meeting with Him is exactly what I need the most.

But God

Remember when I started leading at that prophetic church and didn't realize that they expected me to be meeting with God in private worship throughout the week, not just when I showed up to lead? Let's get into that a little bit. What I didn't realize at the time was that how you show up to lead (or participate in) corporate times of worship is very different from how you show up in your personal times of worship. Corporate worship is not the place to process your pain onstage.

Now, I'm not suggesting ignoring or denying your feelings or frustrations or very real suffering. I'm not asking you to just robotically say "thank you" and praise God while leaving the rest of your emotions behind. In fact, we know from the Psalms that David didn't hide his feelings from the Lord! He wrote and sang things like, "Where are you God? Did you leave me? My enemies surround me!"

Of course, just like David, we need to let it all out and lay it at his feet. Often, that process looks like a lot of tears and giving Him our disappointments and fears. As we give all the ugly stuff to Him, our cries will start to change, and the prayer might become something like, "But God, I know You will come through. You have been faithful before, so You will be faithful again!" If you look at the Psalms, you'll see this happen with David often.

Feeling free to share your mess before God is absolutely necessary. He already knows it's there, so bringing it to Him allows Him to respond and carry it with you or for you. However, this process needs to be done privately—not when you're leading a congregation in worship.

Why? Let me give you an example. Imagine you just walked into a church service for the first time, and I got up on the stage and started singing, "God, I don't know where you are. You have left me in my greatest time of need. I feel broken and lost, and I need Your help! God don't leave me!" What would you be thinking? Could you join me in singing that song? Unless you were in the exact place as me, you probably wouldn't. You might even feel sorry for me or embarrassed, confused by my complaining. Heck, you might even be considering that my complaint is in opposition to God's Word, which says that He'll never leave or forsake us! That lament would have you more focused on me and my feelings instead of God and who He says He is.

The moment ultimately becomes about me and is not helping to corporately put our eyes on Jesus. I wouldn't read my complaints to my boss at a banquet in honor of him, so why would I air out my complaints at the banquet we're throwing for Jesus?

Like David, we should bring our frustrations, confusion, and disappointments to the Lord. Jesus paid for them—and already knows they are there—we just need to know *when* and *where* to bring them.

Bring Everything to the Source

While we're on the topic of grumbling and complaining, I have an interesting question to ponder. Why do you think God disciplined the Israelites for complaining to Moses in the desert, but He never seemed to get after King David for complaining in the Psalms? What was the difference? I believe the difference had everything to do with *who they complained to* rather than *what they were complaining about.*

First of all, God, in His infinite patience, did not discipline the Israelites after they complained about the plagues, the Red Sea, the first bitter waters, the manna, or the quail. God knew that they needed Him, and He came through with some crazy impossible miracles like parting the Red Sea, raining down manna from Heaven to feed them every day, and giving them water from a rock in the desert. He *wanted* to come through for them. He wanted to provide all that they needed, but they still grumbled and complained to each other or Moses, never bringing their requests to God himself! Moses even had to tell them, "Your grumbling is not against us but against the Lord." (Exodus 16:8)

I actually think we do this a lot as His people today. We often blame our spouses, parents, or friends for the situations we find ourselves in because we forget that God is our provider, leader, and protector. God wanted to be that close to His people then, and He still does now. However, a few chapters later, the Israelites tell Moses, "You speak to us, and we will listen; but do not let God speak to us, lest we die." (Exodus 20:19) They did not want to go directly to God. They wanted a mediator. Sadly, that generation was known for grumbling and complaining instead of trusting the Lord, and they got stuck in their wilderness.

But when you start reading some of the Psalms, it does sound like David is complaining! Take a look at a few:

> *"Hear my voice, O God, in my complaint."* (Psalms 64:1)

> *"O God you have rejected us..."* (Psalms 60:1)

> *"My God, my God, why have you forsaken me?"* (Psalms 22:1)

However, notice who David is bringing His complaints to. He is bringing them directly to the One who can answer. Interestingly enough, every single one of those Psalms I mentioned ends on a different note than where they started. Like I mentioned earlier, when we bring our issues to the Lord, He has a way of turning them around so we can remind ourselves of what is actually true.

When David strengthened himself in the Lord, it started with an honest confession of where he was and how he was feeling. But God doesn't leave him there! And He won't leave you in your mess, either. It may not be an immediate answer, but He will change you *and* your perspective if you keep bringing your cares and heart directly to Him.

Like David, we have to bring everything to the source—Jesus. When we grumble and complain to everyone around us, and they likely can't change any of the circumstances, our talk becomes poisonous like gossip. It spreads seeds of doubt and tries to bring other people into the grumbling without going to One who knows every detail of the situation and can actually change things.

I'm sure we all know that gossip can hurt people, but I believe it hurts God as well. The Israelites, in a sense, were spreading doubt and character slander like gossip throughout the community, saying, "Is God with us or is He not?" However, David brought his worries, cares, and fears to God directly, and by the end of the complaint session, the complaining was transformed into praise! We have to exchange our grumbling to other people like the Israelites for bringing an honest offering to God like David.

Here is a practical example of this played out in marriage. Let's say my husband made a comment to me in passing that hurt my feelings. I didn't say anything at first, but later, I start to stew on it. "What did he mean by that? Well, he always does this, and I hate it when he does that." Then, instead of going to him, I go to my best friend and vent.

"Michael said [insert this thing that really hurt me], and I'm so upset. How could he do that?" She takes my side because it's the only one she's heard, so, of course, she's upset at Michael as well. I feel justified in my feelings, yet Michael is not there to defend himself. He becomes the bad guy in this situation, and I'm the victim.

After a while, my husband sees that I'm angry and asks about it, and I finally tell him what he did to hurt me. He explains the situation and apologizes, and in reality, the situation wasn't really what it seemed. We make up, and we are good.

Well, here is the sad part. My friend is left with a tainted view of Michael based on my limited perspective. I brought her my misunderstanding before I brought it to the one who actually had an answer and could speak to the problem.

Doesn't that sound a lot like the Israelites? Wouldn't it have been better if they brought their frustrations up with God Himself so He could remind them of all the miraculous things He had already done for them and bring their perspective back into right view?

My husband and I actually have a rule to not ever bring issues that we have with each other to anyone else unless we have brought them to each other first. If we still need counsel after that first step, we will talk through who we are both okay with bringing our issues to in order to get help. Counsel is good, but bringing it to the source first helps us keep our primary connection and honors the relationships we have with others. I believe it is the same with the Lord.

Stewarding the Heart

As we start to wrap up, I want to talk a little more about the heart of a worshipper. Earlier, we talked about how thanksgiving and praise opens the heart and saw that there truly does seem to be a link between open hearts and open heavens. That being said, one of the greatest ways the enemy gets us to *close* our hearts is through comparison, impatience, hope deferred, and disappointment.

No matter if the call is to be a worship leader, a business owner, a pastor, or a stay-at-home mom, there is often a wrestle with the timing between the call and the desire fulfilled. When it doesn't happen in our timing, we can feel confused or frustrated. Not to mention when other people are promoted around you when you have been waiting longer, are more talented, or have more experience! I believe one of the enemy's greatest strategies is to get us to start pitting ourselves against each other and to start questioning if God really sees us.

I want to share a quick story about a moment I heard a bizarre phrase ringing through my head: "You would be miserable!"

I was sitting in my car, seething with anger after another girl got an opportunity I thought I was a shoo-in for. *Why was she chosen to go to LA to tour with them?! I already paid my dues. I've been singing professionally for five years already!* My face turned hot as all the thoughts kept spiraling. I had worked harder than her, showed up earlier, and given 100 percent every time I had the chance. But her? She was always late, her parents paid for everything, and she was barely 16. Why did she get the opportunity while I was passed over again?

As tears ran down my cheeks, I started the car. I think I had turned on a sermon or interview when a phrase popped suddenly into my head: "You would be miserable in her plan." *What?!* It played in my head again and again like a refrain.

"You would be miserable in her plan."

I was stunned. God had a plan for her life, and it wasn't my plan. If I tried to do what she was doing, I would be miserable. It was as if the blinders fell off of my eyes and a weight dropped off my shoulders. In that moment, I was free. I was no longer competing with anyone else. I knew God had a plan for me, and that was enough. After hearing that simple phrase, I was suddenly free to be happy for her instead of being jealous of her opportunity.

So, let me say this to you: You will be miserable in any plan except the one God has for *you*. He knows the plans He has for *you*. Isn't that freeing?! We don't have to wrestle someone else for a position. He has a plan, and we can trust that we have the grace to walk out our plan with Him. We just don't have the grace for someone else's plan.

I know it's hard to truly walk out, especially when people's highlight reels are posted all over social media. We can see the person in a position that we feel called to and see their life unfold before our very eyes. And, in an odd way, it's a lot like David's waiting season. He slays a giant with a sling and a stone, and everyone is in awe. However, what they didn't see were the lion and the bear David had to slay in secret. They don't see the hours of tending sheep in the fields in all kinds of weather or the hours in the far-away pasture playing and singing his heart out to God. Not to mention the rejection of not even being considered to be a part of the family when a prophet comes to anoint one of your brothers as king! Then, when he was finally anointed and promised the position of king one day, he still had to wait.

When we see somebody's success on a screen or around us at church, we don't see the process that led them there. And, maybe more importantly, we don't realize the weight that comes with it. On the other side of that coin, however, there are those who are promoted prematurely, either for their talent or for their marketing skills. They are at the top, the lights are bright, and exposure is exposing. The hard truth is that when we're in the spotlight or on a stage prematurely, we have to maintain it in our own strength, which can be exhausting to say the least. We feel the pressure to come up with the next hit song or find the next viral thing, and it will never be enough.

Let me tell it to you straight: You will never have enough followers on social media, enough spins on Spotify, or enough praise from man to keep you satisfied if you're living for the applause. This is where we often see burnout or moral failures occur. We may have been exalted for our talent, but we don't have the grace or maturity to maintain and carry it. If Heaven isn't carrying it with us, fame or success are impossible burdens to carry.

Even promotion that is *from* the Lord is impossible to carry without daily dependence! Trusting God's process and timing for promotion is essential. Remember, God has a custom-made path for each of us—one that will confront all of our fears, unbelief, and ability. A path that, if we say "yes" to it, will probably not look like what we think. But, just like David, it will often be perfect training for what the Lord has called you to. That "yes" is still costly.

I don't know if you've noticed this, but I don't think I have ever read a Psalm that said, "God, please do what You promised and make me King." In fact, I know there isn't one, because his goal was never the position. His goal was to be connected to God. David, in a position where his enemies surround him, doesn't ask God to save him so that he can be King. He says something to the effect of, "Save my life. How could I praise you from the grave?" (Psalm 6:5)

David was a worshipper through and through. He had songs in the fields, songs of praise when he was delivered, and songs for help in the caves running from his enemies, just to name a few. His songs were not for platforms but for connection, and we are still connecting and relating to God through David's songs. David didn't ask for his position. He asked to be near to God. Then, in turn, God placed him where he needed to be when he needed to be there.

In fact, I have a similar story.

I was at a worship conference for the first time after having that encounter where God called me His worshipper. After that encounter, I happily laid down my desire for secular music, fame, acting, or anything other than worship, and I was ready to dive in. The problem was, I really didn't know how to get started. I had been a professional singer for about seven years at this point but I didn't know where to even start in the worship space. I remember wanting to talk to the worship band that was leading the conference, but I didn't want to be "that person." You know, the one who was like, "Hi guys, I sing. How do I do what you guys are doing?" So, I just worshipped in the back, not knowing a soul except for Michael.

While in worship, I felt the Lord prompt me to dance. Now, I was definitely not nearly as free as I am now, and the request to dance in a church setting felt really uncomfortable for me. To make matters worse, I felt even more awkward in the row I was standing in. I thought if I started to dance, the whole place would see me and my discomfort. I'm not sure how long this back-and-forth in my head went on, but the worship time ended, and I didn't dance.

Heartbroken by the conviction, I offered up a simple prayer. "Sorry, Lord. If worship starts again, I'll dance." Wouldn't you know it, the speaker gets up, talks for a minute, then asks the band to come back onstage. My heart sank and leapt at the same time! I knew it was my chance to obey. I decided to go up to the front where people had actually been dancing so that when worship started, I had no excuses. I made my way to the front as the speaker asked the band for a specific song, which they didn't know.

By that time, I was standing at the front, and the speaker looked around and asked the entire room, "Does anyone know this specific song?" I sheepishly raised my hand because I *did* know the song, and he called me onstage to sing it. So, I started singing the song, and the band picked it up and started to play behind me. The rest was a blur. The band invited me to have lunch with them after we were done, and they all talked about how they thought that song was gonna be a total disaster because nobody knew if I could actually sing or not. We all laughed together and I was in awe that God initiated the conversation with the band that I was too embarrassed to engage in on my own.

I'll never forget what Lord spoke to me when I got offstage: "If you follow me, I will put you where you need to be when you need to be there."

I didn't go up to the front to sing; I went up there to obey his request for me to dance. Still, my "yes"—even though it was delayed, but praise God for His patience for second chances—put me up front as a worshipper and opened up the doors for the conversation I longed for.

This moment marked me! Any time I have felt the need to strive for a position or a place, He reminds me of that "yes." If I simply trust God and follow Him, even when it's uncomfortable, He will place me where I need to be! And I know He will do the same for you.

King David had many opportunities to try to "help" God make his promise happen. There were many times he could have tried to take the position himself. Even when he was hiding from Saul in a cave, and his right-hand man told him that God had given Saul into his hands, David said, "I will not touch the Lord's anointed." He chose the highest form of trust to let God fulfill his promise to Him and allow God to place him in the position of King.

When God Himself establishes you, you are established with His power and grace. And David and his throne was established *forever*. In fact, Jesus still sits on the throne of David! I truly believe that because David trusted God to fulfill His promise, eternity was impacted.

We don't have to fight and strive for our place and position, we simply have to say "yes" to what He asks us to do and trust that He will make a way where there is no way.

So, as we start to wrap this thing up, remember
that I'm not just speaking to worship leaders here: I'm speaking to YOU. Whatever season you might be in, and whatever it is that you feel called to do, you can assume the posture of worship and approach every situation with an open heart to receive from Heaven.

Amen?!

CONCLUSION

YOU MADE IT! Our prayer as you finish up these last few paragraphs is *not* that you would just feel more equipped as a worship leader or songwriter, or that you would drop everything to move somewhere like Dallas to be part of a church like UPPERROOM— although some of you may very well be walking away from this with one of those things. Our prayer is that your heart would be more open to the Lord in everything you do and that you would understand the power of praise, celebration, and thanksgiving in every part of your life.

In all that we have learned over the last 17 years of seeking out what it looks like to worship God, I feel that we are just scratching the surface. What you've just read about the unveiling of what God meant when He told us that "it's all about worship" is just the tip of the iceberg! The good news is that we are *all* invited into the depths of God that unfold as we continue to ask Him for revelation. That means YOU!

As we continue this ancient journey into the heart of worship, we can't forget we are worshipping a person with real feelings and emotions! He isn't a formula. Yes, he has revealed a clear path to open our hearts through gratitude and praise, which seems to open the corresponding gates of Heaven, but even more than that, it's also an invitation to know His *heart*.

There are ebbs and flows in our relationship as the years go on, but the bottom line is that we cannot learn how to go deeper in worship without learning more about Him! He is a relational God who is inviting us to say "yes" to fully yielding ourselves to Him, and in return, He will take us deeper into His heart—*forever!*

Worship is intended to continue into eternity, and we want to bring as much of Heaven's worship to earth as possible. We pray that what you have read and gleaned from these pages unlocks a hunger to ask God to reveal His secrets to you, too. May your heart *and*

the gates of Heaven open wide for all to experience the
beauty of the King of kings.

Now, go on and praise Him!

MEREDITH MAULDIN is a passionate worshipper and songwriter that can't help pull the song and worship out of others. She spent seven years pioneering the worship and songwriting culture at the UPPERROOM in Dallas and was the founder of their label and publishing company. Meredith has now created a ministry called Songlab Music to empower worshippers to minister to the Lord as well as write songs from their hearts and for their local churches. She has held over 46 SongLabs all over the country since 2019, and releases collective worship music from those events. She is also a voice actor and has most notably played the character of Android 18 in Dragon Ball Z for the last 20 years. She loves hanging with her husband Michael and their three kids! They currently live in Atlanta, GA.

MICHAEL MAULDIN is a husband, father, ordained minister, former model, and film producer. Before stepping into filmmaking, he was the executive director of a worship and prayer movement in Dallas called UPPERROOM. His passion for highlighting the power of worship as a way to transform culture extended from his time as a minister to his films. As a filmmaker, his desire is to impact culture, bending it toward Heaven, but his primary responsibility is raising his three world changers: Ellia, Jon, and Noah Brave.

SONGLAB

If you're a worshipper or songwriter looking to connect and both learn practical tools for writing and delve deeper into the personal nature of praise, we want to invite you to check out SongLab!

What is a SongLab?

A SongLab is a workshop designed to help equip and inspire believers to write and steward the songs the Lord has placed inside their hearts, churches, or communities. During the workshop we give the "why" behind the command to "sing a new song to the Lord," practical training to build out and finish songs, as well as teaching about navigating co-writing with a culture of honor. Our heart is to help inspire a healthy culture of celebration instead of competition. Then, finally, we write, share, and celebrate the songs! Since 2019, we have held over 47 Songlabs, equipped hundreds of worshipers, and written hundreds of beautiful songs! Will you join us next time?

For more information, check out our website
or social media:

www.MauldinMinistries.org
or
www.SonglabMSC.com

Instagram:
@Songlabmsc
@meredithmauldin
@smichaelmauldin

For any questions or booking information:
michael@mauldinmedia.io

There are so many people in our lives that supported us along this journey.

The gratitude begins in our family. We want to give a big THANK YOU to our parents who through their support and belief in us, we are able to recklessly follow God: Steve and Sheilah, Fred and Beverly, Rebecca, Jaan, and Daddy Doug in Heaven!

I also want to thank those who helped make this book happen. Katie Rios for your selfless editing skills! Pete and Rebecca Cartwright for your generosity that gave us the faith to move forward in many ways! George and Ruth Brandon who encouraged us to get our message out. Michael and Lorisa Miller for championing us and giving space for this message to mature and impact a community and thus the world.

Thank you to all of the ministries, churches, and individuals who have lent us their hearts and ears as we've done our best to reflect the heart of Jesus in our words, music, and art.

We love you all.

—MICHAEL and MEREDITH MAULDIN

ENDNOTES

1. Haensch, Anna. "When Choirs Sing, Many Hearts Beat as One." NPR, 10 July 2013, www.npr.org/sections/health-shots/2013/07/09/200390454/when-choirs-sing-many-hearts-beat-as-one.

2. TodayShow. "Gratitude Is Good for Your Health." TODAY.com, November 24, 2021. https:// www.today.com/health/be-thankful-science-says-gratitude-good-your-health-t58256

3. Madhuleena Roy Chowdhury, BA. "The Neuroscience of Gratitude and Effects on the Brain." PositivePsychology.com, October 3, 2023. https://positivepsychology.com/neuroscience-of-gratitude/.